Come and See

Come and See

Come and See

A 30-day Devotional of John 1

DAMARIS U. AVILA

RESOURCE *Publications* · Eugene, Oregon

COME AND SEE
A 30-day Devotional of John 1

Resource Publications
An Imprint of Wipf and Stock Publishers
199 W. 8th Ave., Suite 3
Eugene, OR 97401

www.wipfandstock.com

PAPERBACK ISBN: 978-1-5326-4394-1
HARDCOVER ISBN: 978-1-5326-4395-8
EBOOK ISBN: 978-1-5326-4396-5

Manufactured in the U.S.A.   MARCH 12, 2019

To Tachu, Arianne and Sophie

CONTENTS

CONTENTS

PERMISSIONS

ACKNOWLEDGMENTS

To my patient and loving husband, Tachu, thank you for your endless support with this project. Thank you for believing that I had a story to tell worth writing about. You listen and you care and you always lend me your ear. To know that I have your ear and my Father's ear, is to be seen and loved. You are a gift.

To Arianne, thank you for teaching me what it means to be a mom, to feel your love and care and concern for my well being. Thank you that you have loved me in the best way possible. May you know that the story He is writing in your life, is worth sharing with those around you. May He always be your source of strength that in Him you would have unwavering faith and unswerving hope. May His Word carry you through every high and low until the day we walk into heavens gates.

To Sophie, I carry with me sweet memories of you checking in on me throughout this project, genuinely concerned and interested in the words written in my heart. Your hugs, smiles and prayers for me, are a true gift from heaven. May your sweet and tender heart hold His love and truth as the most precious treasure in this life, that when you walk heavens gates, you will see His love and truth face-to-face.

To Papito, thank you for your fierce love toward your daughters and grandchildren. Thank you for teaching me loyalty and love in the joys of everyday life. Your devoted heart has taught me the true essence of fatherly love. Your support and embrace have carried me through some of the darkest times of my life. I would not be who I am without you.

To my Mamita Linda, what joys this life has brought me through your life. Thank you for your constant support, your relentless prayers and your fierce faith. Thank you for introducing us to Jesus. His grace, mercy and sacrificial love. You've taught me the Way, my most treasured gift. And now, you teach my girls. Our family would not be where we are without your prayers.

To my sisters, thank you for praying and encouraging me through a journey I've never walked before. From our childhood joys to our lives as adults and mothers, your love has been a constant reminder to push forward.

To my prayer warrior friends, thank you for your care, love and prayers over me as I wrote and discovered the words in my heart. Your sincere love is a gift from heaven I will forever treasure in my heart.

To Julia, my teacher, mentor, sister and friend. You gave me the courage I needed to write. Your profound teaching of His Word and your dedication to His truths, impacted my life in more ways than one. You taught me to love His Word and to not keep it to myself. Thank you for reading my very first manuscript and for helping guide and direct my writing. I am forever grateful to you.

To Brian, a million thank you's for all of your time and energy spent reading and editing my manuscript. Thank you for your dedication to excellence and nothing less. Thank you for encouraging me to persevere in the world of writing. You encouraged me the whole way through.

To my home church, CPC, your dedication to make and mature followers of Christ is the very essence of who you are. After being absent for a decade, I walked into the church famished and thirsty. Your teaching fed me and nurtured me back to health and continues to do so. Jesus is the great Physician and He continually uses you to heal the areas of my heart that are most broken. Thank you for your unwavering dedication to grace and truth.

Introduction

"For the Son of Man came to seek and to save what was lost."
LUKE 19:10

ABOUT THE BOOK:

COME AND SEE IS a project that started many years ago during a
time of quiet and heartfelt meditation on Jesus' words. It started
out as a compilation of journal entries and poignant truths that
jumped out of the very pages of the book of John. It has turned
out to be my heart's greatest passion, putting together a thirty-day
devotional study, verse by verse, of John 1. As you study a verse
each day, I have interwoven applicable, very personal testimonies
of my faith and journey with Jesus. I share the highs along with the
very real struggles and disappointments where God has met me
and lifted me up. My desire is that through the work of the Holy
Spirit, each verse will come alive in your hearts. I hope and pray
that this book will draw you closer to His heart. That it will lead
you to come into His presence every day and see Jesus.

ABOUT THE AUTHOR, THE APOSTLE JOHN:

The apostle John walked with Jesus during His ministry that lasted
approximately three and a half years. He was a beloved and devout apostle and follower of Christ. He walked and talked with
our LORD. The apostle John takes us on a journey where we learn

what it means to walk alongside Jesus. He simultaneously teaches us the realities of this dark world as well as the hope that abounds in our Savior, Jesus Christ. John's narrative is not one of storytelling as much as it is of truth-telling. He invites you into God's story that you might find yourself in it and more importantly, see Jesus.

ABOUT JOHN THE BAPTIST:

Not to be confused with the apostle John, John the Baptist is Jesus' cousin, born approximately six months before Jesus. His mother, Elizabeth, is a relative of Mary, the mother of Jesus. One of the very first things said about John the Baptist is during Mary's visit to Elizabeth (both were pregnant at the time), "When Elizabeth heard Mary's greeting, the baby leaped in her womb, and Elizabeth was filled with the Holy Spirit" (Luke 1:41). The first encounter John the Baptist had with his cousin Jesus is remarkable. This marks the beginning of John the Baptist's calling and purpose in preparing the way for hearts to listen and accept the saving grace of Jesus. John the Baptist was a devout believer in Christ even before he saw him with his own eyes. He went around sharing and exalting the coming Messiah, the long-awaited Savior of the Jews and, we would learn, non-Jews. His gift was for all to receive.

HOW TO READ THROUGH THIS DEVOTIONAL BOOK:

The book is intended to be read as a daily devotional study. It is divided into chapters or days with the intent of reading it as a 30-day journey inviting you to come and see the truth about Jesus.

Day: Each day begins with a very personal short story of how God has impressed upon me the importance of the verse for that day. It ends with a short phrase, something you can take away with you to remember the story and apply its teaching to your life.

Come and See: Following the short story, you are invited to come and see Jesus in John 1. We begin in verse 1 on Day 1 and continue through each verse, in order, until we reach the end with verse 51 on Day 30. You will find each verse written out for you right below the Come and See title for each day, so you are able to follow along. Additionally, where necessary, I have added verses from the Bible to help further explain my teaching.

At the end of each devotion, you will find a section titled:

Prayer: Suggests a prayer if it is your heart's desire.

Reflect: Allows for some reflection time on the reading and taking action toward change.

His Word: Allows you the opportunity to memorize and draw His teaching closer to your heart.

~ One ~

I Now Know Who I Am Because of "I AM"

As a young child I certainly had not grasped the intensity of this truth: His breath is in me. I battled with my outer appearance which I believed only served to expose my inner inadequacies: my dark brown skin and black stringy hair all pointed to the "language barrier" in my home. I so longed to be like everyone else around me; to have an identity grounded in commonality.

But because I was raised in what you could call cultural dualism (raised and influenced by two cultures), I was neither American, nor Guatemalan. I couldn't see that I was both, but only felt that I was neither. The trips to Central America only reminded me of how American I truly was. The American history classes and the holiday traditions at school only reminded me of how Guatemalan I truly felt. How easy it is to see what we aren't instead of what we are, and to then feel isolated and lost in the chasm between two worlds.

But as I lean into the Word of God, I see the beauty in my reality because of who He is, beauty so profound it penetrates my heart and soul. I learn that Christ's identity as God and Creator defines my identity. He is my God and my Creator, therefore I am His child and His creation. How's that for dualism? I am both, so this makes me 100 percent His. My newfound identity is in Jesus. I am forever, lavishly rich as His child and creation. I can fully embrace my identity because of His. So I learn that who I am is not how I look or how I speak, but who I am is defined by who He is.

I now know who I am because of "I AM."

COME AND SEE

In the beginning was the Word, and the Word was with God, and the Word was God. He was with God in the beginning. Through him all things were made; without him nothing was made that has been made.
(John 1:1–3)

What if I told you that the most unbelievable reality for you and me entered our lives thousands of years ago? That's right, our reality was forever established before we took our first breath. Someone we can call Savior, King, Prince of peace, Creator of the world, existed before time, before the earth's formation. Jesus was present and the conduit by which the earth was formed and created. He was there when all was but mere emptiness. An empty canvas that had yet to taste the beauty of His voice, His breath. The Word spoke and the earth came to be. God breathed and our souls came alive.

The One who calls Himself the great "I AM" was in all His glory, giving life to an unimaginable creation. "The Word," as today's verse calls Him, spoke life into all that He created, out of nothing. The Word is Jesus, and there is no illusion as to where Jesus was at the beginning. "I AM" was with God and He is God. He is and He was and He will forever be the Great "I AM."

> God said to Moses, "I AM WHO I AM. This is what you are to say to the Israelites: 'I am has sent me to you.'" (Exodus 3:14)
> "Very truly I tell you," Jesus answered, "before Abraham was born, I am!" (John 8:58)

If we go back to the beginning in Genesis, we see that it begins with God speaking and all of creation in utter obedience coming to be at the sound of His voice. Let's read it together in Genesis 1:

> "In the beginning God created the heavens and the earth" (v. 1).
>
> "And God *said, 'Let there be* light (v. 3) . . . *Let there be* a vault between the waters (v. 6) . . . *Let* the water under the sky be gathered to one place (v. 9) . . . *Let* the land produce vegetation (v. 11) . . . *Let there be* lights in the vault of the sky (v. 14) . . . *Let* the water teem with living creatures (v. 20) . . . *Let* the land produce living creatures according to their kinds (v. 24) . . . *Let* us make mankind in our image, in our likeness'" (v. 26)

Place yourself in this beginning that Genesis speaks of. The beginning of your story with all of creation: day, night, skies, sun, moon, stars, animals, plants, and seas. This is God's narrative, and because He sees the end from the beginning we are in it. We are in Adam and Eve's gene pool.

The Word, who created everything and everyone, thought of you at the very beginning. You were never an afterthought, but a love, a life that He honored by breathing life into you and making you in His own image - to rule over all that He had created. To enjoy it, care for it, love on it.

> Then God said, "Let us make mankind in our image, in our likeness, so that they may rule over the fish in the sea and the birds in the sky, over the livestock and all the wild animals, and over all the creatures that move along the ground." So God created mankind in his own image, in the image of God he created them; male and female he created them. (Genesis 1:26–27)

Dear Father,
Thank You that You are 100 percent mine, my God and my
Creator. Help me to remember that my identity is tied to Yours.
Help me to see myself as You see me, through Your eyes. Help me
to see myself in light of Your Word.
In Jesus' Name, Amen.

Reflect ~

Do you see yourself in God's narrative? Do you believe He is writing your story? Take some time to think about what this means.

His Word ~

The earth is the LORD's, and everything in it,
The world, and all who live in it;
For he founded it on the seas
and established it on the waters. (Psalm 24:1–2)

~ *Two* ~

WHEN HIS LIGHT GIVES YOU LIFE, YOUR LIFE GIVES OTHERS LIGHT

MY FATHER PACED THE living room that morning. It was odd for me. I never knew a man more extroverted, hospitable, and willing to share with others. Yet this public speaking engagement proved to be different for him. By invitation of my daughter and her fourth grade class, he would be sharing his journey from Guatemala to the US forty-six years ago. He retraced the memories in his head as he rehearsed hours before the panel that day.

That afternoon began with a permeable sentiment, the children fully enthralled by all the heroic and emotional stories that had been shared by the other panelists. As the attention turned to my father, his smirk revealed the sweet yet mischievous anecdotes that had yet to be shared. His was not a story of war-torn Guatemala, or even economic hardship. His was a story of romantic love. A true story of two teenagers, their long-lost love, and the journey that led to their reunion in a land that was foreign to both of them: U.S.A.

Love, a far-away journey, and a candy factory were all themes the children ate up. As he shared his story, my father found himself reminiscing about the day that changed his life forever. The moment he found himself at the doorstep of his future wife's (my mother's) apartment, thousands of miles from where they first met. My mother, after finding herself on her knees in her L.A. apartment, praying for a reunion, would open the door to find my father standing there, at her doorstep. A divine appointment, a miracle right before her very eyes in the City of Angels.

To understand this better, let me go back to the beginning. After falling in love in Guatemala two years prior, my mother and father were separated by more than a 3,000-mile divide. My mother was uprooted from the only country and language she knew. She was taken to Los Angeles to study and work alongside my grandmother, leaving behind her brothers and sisters, family, friends, and not the least, the man she loved.

Despite my father not sharing every detail that afternoon (though the fourth graders would have loved it), the very miraculous nature of his story struck him yet again. He couldn't help but end his time of sharing by thanking God for His unwavering love and faithfulness to a young couple. In the end, not knowing that a daughter who looked exactly like him would be on the other side of that apartment door, he searched for love and was given the gift of life: a one-year-old daughter.

Often we fail to see God's light shining within our very imperfect lives; His light, our lifeline that directs our path in life. It takes us to the unexpected, to what we don't deserve but so happily receive. His life is our very oxygen that keeps us going during those difficult days of struggle and loss because God does not demand perfection, but rather invites imperfect souls to follow His perfect light.

When His light gives you life,
your life gives others light.

COME AND SEE

In him was life, and that life was the light of all mankind.
(JOHN 1:4)

It's hard to imagine that a single being could ever enter earth embodying eternal life—not in need of being rescued from death or healed from disease. Yet Jesus came as the all-conquering God, fully filled with the Spirit. Though Jesus came with all the physical human characteristics you and I possess—hunger, thirst, sleep and emotion—He did not have sin. In reality, He was perfect. Life was within Him and His light was our lifeline. And there wasn't anyone or anything that could take that away from Him. Not even death. He defied death, not by staying alive, but by conquering it. He faced death, battled hell, and won!

Jesus' life on earth was not one of daily survival but one of daily living because life was found in Him. And this life was the light for me and you, meaning He came as the light that leads us day by day, that brightens the darkest areas of our lives, that shines through the darkest, most insecure crevices and holes of our hearts. Light that warms the coldest parts of our souls during the most difficult seasons of life. Light that shines love and redemption even in the most sinful seasons of life. He is the light that we all so desperately need to survive—no, to live. Because through Him, we too can ultimately defy death, the death of merely surviving and not living.

Dear Father,
Thank You that Your very light is my lifeline. Thank You that when I seek You, You give me the gift of Your presence. Please give me eyes to see the story You are writing in my life. Give me eyes to see Your fingerprints in the tapestry of my life.
In Jesus' Name, Amen.

Reflect ~

What story is He writing in your life? Sometimes we just need a moment to stop and think about it to really see it. Do you see it? Ask Him to show you and then Thank Him for what He's doing in your life.

His Word ~

The Son is the radiance of God's glory and the exact representation of his being, sustaining all things by his powerful word. (Hebrews 1:3a)

~ *Three* ~

HE PURSUED ME EVEN
INTO DARKNESS

AT ONE POINT IN my life I became an expert at suppressing His light. It appeared in the dark places of my life, but I always ran, not wanting to be found. I could hear His gentle whispers deep in my heart, but I failed to acknowledge them. Oh, how I lost precious years serving the idol of "me." Sure, I attended church most Sundays as if to appease Him. I suppose I thought checking it off my list for the week was enough. How far I had drifted. But His profound love never stopped pursuing me.

I specifically remember one morning sitting in one of the pews in the back of the church. I was living in Central America at the time and felt content finding an American church that led their Sunday morning service with hymns, prayers, and a blessing. There was an element of "home" at this church. How unfortunate that it had little to do with God and more to do with language and tradition. It was something I knew and could easily fall into a pattern of attending, singing, nodding, reading, and agreeing, as if the church gods were looking down on me in approval. But I remember this one particular morning walking out of church still feeling so empty.

It was no longer about being in church, but entirely about going to church. It was no longer about staying in church but entirely about getting in and out quickly. So every Sunday I could sneak in late and slip out early and no one would ever notice. And nobody did. I had completely missed the point of being in church.

Though I only called on His name when I was desperate, He ran to me each and every time. His love so unstoppable, He pursued me. I was just too selfish and embarrassed to see it at the time. And though I avoided some sins, I walked right into others. But He so graciously called me by name and saved me from the selfish life I had chosen. He was patient with me and still is. His light shone in my darkness, and the pit of darkness I was in never overcame His light.

He pursues me even into darkness.
He reclaims me.
He redeems me.
He restores me.

COME AND SEE

The light shines in the darkness,
and the darkness has not overcome it.
(JOHN 1:5)

Have you ever seen the sun's bright rays piercing through on a cloudy day? It's as if the clouds are racing to block the sun, yet the sun's light always comes through even if it is only between two clouds. As I imagine this, I think about the light that Jesus is and how His light pierced through a dark world when He came to us. Like the sun, His light shone between two groups that opposed Him (the Romans and the Jews).

Jesus Christ, the Creator of all mankind, created us to have an understanding of this light within. He left His fingerprints in each and every one of us, His "Handmade by God" brand in our souls. This was His purpose, to come to us and leave us with this great gift. And through His death, we gained His light.

> Again Jesus spoke to them, saying, "I am the light of the
> world. Whoever follows me will not walk in darkness,
> but will have the light of life." (John 8:12 ESV)

But though He came to His people, they did not see Him. They
were unable to see the Light of the world because of their blind-
ness. They neither accepted nor received Him as their own, as their
Savior, as their Messiah. They did not comprehend the Light. The
Messiah they longed for was among them and they totally missed
Him.

As Matthew Henry put it: "The world of mankind compre-
hended not the natural light that was in their understandings, but
became vain in their imaginations concerning the eternal God and
the eternal Word, Rom. 1:21, 28. The darkness of error and sin
overpowered and quite eclipsed this light."[1]

Have you ever observed a solar eclipse? From a quick search
on the NASA website you will notice how the sun is never completely blocked. It's impossible for the sun to fully disappear during
an eclipse. The sun radiates light even when the moon passes in
front of it. In this same way, the enemy attempted to obscure the
light that was in this world, but Jesus' light permeated the earth. So
blindness, animosity, and further rejection of Jesus cannot put this
light out entirely. This is powerful for believers because it proves
that no amount of sin, deceit, hate, or disillusionment can ever
turn Jesus off or away from us.

Dear Father,
Thank You that even when I try and hide, You see me, because
nothing in this world can ever separate me from Your love or
presence. Forgive me for running away from You and suppress-
ing Your light for far too long. I don't want to run from You
anymore. Help me to run to You, toward the light, always.
In Jesus' Name, Amen.

---

1. Henry, "John 1:1," II. 5. (2.).

Reflect ~

Have you been suppressing God's light in your life? Are you ready to let Him in? Share your heart with Jesus today and ask Him to release you from the darkness.

His Word ~

For I am convinced that neither death nor life, neither angels nor demons, neither the present nor the future, nor any powers, neither height nor depth, nor anything else in all creation, will be able to separate us from the love of God that is in Christ Jesus our Lord. (Romans 8:38–39)

~ Four ~

"CHRIST WITH ME, CHRIST BEFORE ME, CHRIST BEHIND ME, CHRIST IN ME"

HER WORDS PENETRATED MY heart and consumed my mind that morning. I could see it in my husband's face too. We fought back tears as voice after voice expressed dark, lonely, and suppressed feelings. And the eloquence and conviction with which they spoke was even more alarming because it was clear that it wasn't just about completing another assignment. No, this was personal and written poetry from the depths of their hearts. The descriptive words and phrases they used described the same loneliness, pain, and darkness that I, and I'm sure other parents present that morning, had experienced. These students got it. They were much too young to know and understand so intimately the woes of life, yet here they were. Expressing their hearts to us through art, these young fourth-graders had changed our lives forever. A morning of poetry reading had quite unsettled us.

We were silent as we walked away that day. But my thoughts raced with questions. How? Why? This was one of those things I would not be able to shake off. So I cried, "God please help these children." But my prayer was returned to me. God was telling me to do something about it. Often we pray for outcomes without realizing that the seed of grace was planted in our hearts because God is saying, "What are you willing to do about it?" But I am just not that brave. What would I do? The "where," the "when," and the "why" were easy. But the "what." That question stared at me for hours.

So I sat in front of my computer with my email open to a blank page. I started typing only to quickly delete every character till it was blank again. I did this several times, I lost count. Finally, after praying, I took a deep breath and simply wrote from my heart. As scared as I was, I knew that God had given me this deep desire to reach out to these girls, and I had to trust that He would bring it together. All I needed to do was invite them. So I emailed the moms in my daughter's class and I shared that I wanted to open our home to host an after-school BeYOUtiful Girl Time. We would learn how specially God had created us, and who He created us to be by first learning who we are in light of who God is. An idea that had come from a desire in my heart was now coming to fruition. A seed was planted. It grew and blossomed. It's an amazing thing—it's life, really—when you see God turn a dark morning into a bright and hopeful future.

BeYOUtiful Girl Time has become a sisterhood for fourth-, fifth-, and sixth-grade girls. The fear of starting a faith-based after-school program almost paralyzed me. And the words of Erwin McManus rang in my ear: oh how "our faith becomes a crutch not a launching pad."[1]

If "Christ with me,
Christ before me,
Christ behind me,
Christ in me,[2]*"*
doesn't catapult me to take risks,
then what will?

1. McManus, "Really!?," 21:31.
2. Patrick, "Saint Patrick Quotes."

COME AND SEE

*There was a man sent from God whose name was John. He
came as a witness to testify concerning that light, so that
through him all might believe. He himself was not the light;
he came only as a witness to the light. The true light that gives
light to everyone was coming into the world.*
(JOHN 1:6–9)

I wonder if you know anyone who fits this description: "his clothes
were made of camel's hair, and he had a leather belt around his
waist. His food was locusts and wild honey" (John 3:4)? An un-
common yet fascinating depiction of a man. This description is of
John the Baptist. John the Baptist was a tough and unambiguous
man of the desert, yet his inner being was all heart and soul. He
was sent to speak to what matters most, to the very essence of why
and for what we were created. Like Isaiah the prophet had foretold
many centuries prior:

> "A voice of one calling: 'In the wilderness prepare the
> way for the LORD; make straight in the desert a highway
> for our God.'" (Isaiah 40:3)

God knows very well what we need at the very moment we need
it. The people needed someone to lead them home, to lead them
to their Savior. So He sent a man of honor, a man of the earth,
one who is sustained by God and His creation. John the Baptist
was the appointed one who would announce and lead the people
to Jesus—dressed in camel's hair and a leather belt, yet clothed in
truth. He was a witness to Jesus and His very nature and purpose
so that everyone would recognize Him and accept Him once He
appeared to them.

And so I am reminded that I am to be a witness to the light,
spreading light everywhere I go, to be a fire of hope to those around
me, to lead them into the arms of our loving Jesus.

Dear Father,
Thank You for sending Your Son, the Light of the world into
my life. Thank You for the people You also sent into my life
to help lead me home. Help me become a person of faith who
shines Your light and helps others find Jesus.
In Jesus' Name, Amen.

Reflect ~

Where is God calling you more deeply to be a light? Let Him work
out the who, what, where, when, why, and how. Ask Jesus to show
you your next step and let Him catapult you into your next dream
and passion where you will lead others to the Light.

His Word ~

For we are God's masterpiece. He has created us anew in Christ
Jesus, so we can do the good things he planned for us long ago.
(Ephesians 2:10)

~ *Five* ~

EYES TO SEE, EARS TO HEAR, HEARTS TO SURRENDER

HAVE YOU EVER THOUGHT about what that first Christmas in Bethlehem was like over 2,000 years ago? What sounds were heard, what activities took place, what meals and scents aroused everyone's palettes? Mainly, was it anything like what some of us celebrate every year on December 25? I want to help you envision what it may have looked like for Mary and Joseph. Maybe, from a slightly different perspective, we can imagine what it was like the night of Jesus' birth.

On that dark and fearful night when Mary carried our Savior in her womb, door after door, knock after knock, she was sent away. The One who invites us in, was not invited in at any inn. The One who makes room for us all was met with no room at all throughout Bethlehem. A crying and desperate Mary carried grace and truth in her womb, and yet, door after door, knock after knock, she was sent away. The One who gives us His warm and gentle heart was met with cold and hostile hearts at every corner.

Upon entering an open door, Mary found herself in the darkest, loudest, dirtiest, most unsightly room of all: a cave, a barn which housed the very animals the Savior in her womb had created. Surrounded by wailing animals, the Baby joined us with a simple cry that penetrated his earthly mother's and father's heart and soul. The first sound of their baby's voice, their Savior's voice, the first touch of His skin, the first warm breath—they treasured all these moments in their hearts as He lay in their arms.

His love for us burned so strong that He left His throne to enter our mess. No amount of sin could keep Him away, so He came to us as a helpless babe. Not destined to be born into royal status here on Earth, He chose to be clothed in regular skin, body, and garments. He didn't demand a crown, a grand entrance, or even a decent place of birth. He imposed His birth on no one. He would not force His gift on anyone, but would offer it to everyone in hopes that we would take Him in.

Oh that we would have
Eyes to see, to recognize Him,
Ears to hear, to know Him,
Hearts to surrender, to receive Him.

COME AND SEE

He was in the world, and though the world was made through him, the world did not recognize him. He came to that which was his own, but his own did not receive him.
(JOHN 1:10–11)

God made us in love and for love, yet we chose no love for Him. He came in love for love, yet we rejected Him. We rejected the One who came to bleed for us all. We turned our ears away from the Voice who spoke the world into being. We turned our eyes away from the One who first set His eyes on us. We turned our voices against the Breath who by His Spirit breathed life into us.

The Son of man took on humanity, leaving His heavenly realm for a time, though never compromising nor leaving His deity behind. Though He came to His creation, He—the Artist, the Creator, the Maker, the Owner of it all—was not accepted or recognized. The very people He designed in love and beauty kicked Him out of His own design. In a story where the king chooses to leave his glorious kingdom to visit the lower world because those he serves need to be saved desperately, should not the king be received with the very best those he serves have to offer? The best of their being to receive and honor the king with praise and admiration?

But in this very true story, Jesus, the King, was thrown out, beaten, flogged, and killed by the very people He served and came to sacrifice Himself for. By the Jews He was born into, by the Romans He designed and created, by His children of all nations He loved and made. Instead of a crown of gold, I gave Him a crown of thorns. Instead of a velvet robe, I removed His clothes. Instead of placing Him on high where the whole of Israel could worship and praise Him, I placed Him on a cross where the whole of Israel could ridicule and scorn Him. Instead of receiving Him with warm and praising hearts, I rejected Him with cold and unremitting remarks. Yet He still chose to sacrifice His life and die an excruciatingly painful death just to lead me home. To open my eyes. As Matthew Henry put it:

> "They had the oracles of God, which told them beforehand when and where to expect him, and of what tribe and family he should arise. He came among them himself, introduced with signs and wonders, and himself the greatest; and therefore it is not said of them, as it was of the world (v. 10), that they knew him not; but his own, though they could not but know him, yet received him not; did not receive his doctrine, did not welcome him as the Messiah, but fortified themselves against him. The chief priests, that were in a particular manner his own (for the Levites were God's tribe), were ring-leaders in this contempt put upon him."[1]

We all sent Him to the cross. But today we can join the likes of those who turned their eyes from Him or join the saints who turned their whole lives toward Him. Which will it be?

---

1. Henry, "John 1:6," II. 3. (1.).

Dear Father,
I have rejected or pushed away Your Son in my life. I have cho-
sen to not believe or to not care. Please forgive me. I now see
that all You have ever done is because of Your immense love
for me. Soften my heart that I may receive Your love. Please
help me remember the ultimate sacrifice You made for my life.
In Jesus' Name, Amen.

Reflect ~

Are you ready to invite Jesus into your heart and into every facet of
your life? He is waiting for you and slowly calls you into Him. Talk
with Him today and let Him settle your unsettled heart.

His Word ~

. . . so Christ was sacrificed once to take away the sins of many; and
he will appear a second time, not to bear sin, but to bring salvation
to those who are waiting for him. (Hebrews 9:28)

~ Six ~

Your Present Reality and
Your Future Eternity

I remember being so smitten by the idea of being born again. To have a second birth seemed so awesome to me. My faith as a young child was vibrant and real. I understood that my heart had been entirely washed, cleansed of all my sins up until that point in my life and for any future disobedience to God. It felt safe and freeing. It became all the more beautiful and real when I was baptized with water at the young age of six. It was an experience I will never forget. I felt Him in such a rich and palpable way.

The day I was baptized is forever in my heart. I was submerged into water and saw the very light from above, angels around me as I was dipped into water and then carried out. How I wished it could have lasted longer. I saw the very glory of our Father, seated in heaven on His throne, a bright light like the sun. It was as if His light were beaming right through our church ceiling, like I had been baptized outside on a bright and sunny day. It was the Spirit of God shining on me. And it was a very personal moment where He saw me and embraced me. My life had been sealed and saved through the blood of Jesus the day I chose to believe and receive Him as my Savior. And on this day, His seal upon my life was revealed in baptism.

I never did talk about what I felt and experienced that day. It is something I have treasured and meditated on in my heart. And now I see it is something that should be celebrated every year, like a birthday. It is a birthday. It is a born-again remembrance, a born-of-God celebration, an everlasting reminder of my King Jesus and the great gift He gave me. An immense gift of forgiveness of sins and forgottenness of sins. A reminder that His resurrection is my resurrection, His ascension is my ascension, His presence with the Father is my presence with the Father.

Your present reality and your future eternity
are all transformed as His sons and daughters.
Your sins to be forgiven and your past forgotten.

COME AND SEE

Yet to all who did receive him, to those who believed in his name, he gave the right to become children of God—children born not of natural descent, nor of human decision or a husband's will, but born of God.
(JOHN 1:12–13)

Do you ever think about your birth? In all honesty, I hadn't thought about it at all until I read and studied these verses. As I thought about my birth, I couldn't help but envision the conversation, mood, and ambiance that led to me being conceived and then born. I suppose it's not something we really want to think about! But having the assurance that I was loved and wanted from the start is a sweet feeling. My parents have reassured me of their love time and time again. Though I do know my father wanted a son he could name Enrique, after his late brother, my father ended up with four daughters, just like his brother. And somehow I think that was sweeter.

I think about the many stories of conception and birth—some funny, some serious, and some not so loveable. This verse leads me to think about man's will and how our actions lead to certain outcomes. Sometimes those outcomes are so unfavorable to those involved, particularly innocent children. As I meditate further on

John's words here, I realize that regardless of what our birth stories are, we are all invited to become part of a new birth. A birth by God's will that is filled with His love and His plans for us that are all good. There is no bad in this narrative. It is only filled with absolute goodness and promises that will never be broken because they are given to us by an oath-keeping, promise-keeping God.

We are children of God through a holy and supernatural birth—conceived in love and truth. Jesus was conceived by the Spirit (placed in Mary's womb) and so are we conceived by the Spirit, through the breath of God. It is not required that we come from the natural lineage of God like our children come from our lineage. This is God's decision to grant us this rebirth if we will take it.

By far, the most important decision we make in our lifetime is how we respond to God's offer of new birth. There are so many things that compete for our attention, things that on their own merit are not wrong things to pursue. However, in the grand scheme of life, how we respond to God's invitation will determine our future here on Earth. But even more, eternity after Earth.

Dear Father,
How is it that You have called me Your child? Thank You for adopting me into Your royal family, into Your kingdom, forever. Thank You for personally loving me. Today and always, help me to celebrate this gift of adoption. I pray that the things of this earth would not take hold of my heart and that I would delight more and more in You.
In Jesus' Name, Amen.

Reflect ~

Who have you chosen to live for? Is it time to reprioritize your life? Take some time to think about this and to open your heart to God about what you would like to change. Ask a friend to come alongside you in prayer.

His Word ~

For he chose us in him before the creation of the world to be holy and blameless in his sight. In love he predestined us to be adopted as his sons through Jesus Christ, in accordance with his pleasure and will—to the praise of his glorious grace, which he has freely given us in the One he loves. (Ephesians 1:4–6)

~ *Seven* ~

He Made His Dwelling among Us

THE FLOODGATES WOULD OPEN every year we dropped my father off at the San Francisco Airport for his annual trip to visit his parents and brothers in Guatemala. As a family, I think we could collectively fill several buckets of tears that day. And the tears continued through the drive home and into the first nights without him. You would think we were saying goodbye forever. But it was a two-week trip that felt like a two-year sabbatical from his family. I know we cried in part because we missed him, but we also wanted to visit our grandparents. Travel back then for our family was a huge luxury and rarity. Every few years my parents took us to Guatemala with them, but due to the high cost of travel, my dad would take us on a six-day road trip to get there. Then of course, the waterworks began in Guatemala days before we would get into our car as a family to head back. We would drive away at dawn as we waved goodbye to our most precious grandma and grandpa as they stood at their front door. Every goodbye was the worst goodbye in the history of goodbyes. Saying goodbye to our family didn't come with a "see you again" date. It would be many years before we saw everyone again. And some we would not see again.

It was extra painful watching my dad cry as he drove away. It does something to a girl when she sees her father broken and inconsolable. What awaited him was a six-day journey. That meant twelve hours a day of roads, trees, highways, gas stations, and his thoughts. As days passed, I don't think it got any easier. With every passing day, he missed his parents even more. It wasn't during an era of cell phones and Facetime. A once-a-month phone call was all they had.

And I think about the pain that results in moving and leaving family. My dad was a devoted father, but the emptiness he felt from being so far from his parents was very present. I think about his sacrifice, leaving the country that he loved with the people that he cherished because that is what was best for our family. And then I wonder, what must it have been like for Jesus to leave His Father? To make this immense move and relocation. And He was going from the promised land, heaven, to the lowly land, Earth. What awaited Him was harsh, brutal, and altogether dark, but he was willing to do this because that is what was best for us.

He made His dwelling among us
that He might make His dwelling within us.

COME AND SEE

The Word became flesh and made his dwelling among us.
(JOHN 1:14A)

When I try to envision Jesus leaving His Father to come to Earth, I wonder what that moment was like. The Father sending His Son to complete a mission impossible that was only possible for Him. The most important mission humanity had ever seen. It's devastating, yet so amazing. I imagine heaven rejoiced and the angels praised and worshipped the Son of God as He departed, sending Him off with angelic song and voices proclaiming "Holy, Holy, Holy." The Father sending His Son that we may all know that He is . . .

"the way and the truth and the life." (John 14:6)

The Word from creation above, Jesus from His presence on high, visited us. Since eternity past, He had never been separated from His Father. And He didn't enter this world in opulence or high status, and He didn't simply descend from the heavens. He entered this world in the same way you and I came into the world, through a painful and long delivery. But He was delivered to us in a most perfect, love-filled package. Wanting to connect with us in every way, He was born of natural descent, through a lineage that traces back to the beginning of time, to the beginning of the Old Testament Scriptures. Yet, He was conceived and born of supernatural powers through the Holy Spirit, and He came into this world in perfect, heavenly embodiment as a man. As J.I. Packer explains it,

> "God became man; the divine Son became a Jew; the Almighty appeared on earth as a helpless human baby, unable to do more than lie and stare and wriggle and make noises, needing to be fed and changed and taught to talk like any other child. And there was no illusion or deception in this: the babyhood of the Son of God was a reality."[1]

Let us reflect on the reality of Jesus on Earth in this short poem:

He *reached* down from heaven above and *touched* us.
His love so profound He *became one of us.*
He *visited* our cities, our homes, and our temples.
He *walked* our streets, our markets with the disciples.
He *entered* our world to draw us out of it,
to enter our hearts and draw us near to Him.
That He might . . .
Forever live in our hearts.
Forever love through our hearts.
Forever light the world from our hearts.

---

1. Packer, *Knowing God*, 53.

Dear Father,
How could I ever thank You for delivering Your Son to me?
For loving me so graciously that You became one of us? Thank
You for showing me through Your pain and suffering that You
understand mine. Thank You for leaving Your throne on high
to come and be near me. Please help me to never forget Your
immense sacrifice for my life, and to remember that I am Your
beloved.
In Jesus' Name, Amen.

Reflect ~

Is it hard to imagine that Jesus loves you so much that He did this
for you? The Bible says that it was His great pleasure and will.
Thank Him with all of your heart for loving you so much to complete this excruciating journey.

His Word ~

Who, being in very nature, God,
did not consider equality with God something to be
used to his own advantage;
rather, he made himself nothing
by taking the very nature of a servant,
being made in human likeness.
and being found in appearance as a man,
he humbled himself
by becoming obedient to death—
even death on a cross! (Philippians 2:6–8)

~ Eight ~

WE HAVE GAINED
THE RICHES OF HIS GLORY

THE DAY MY DAD met his firstborn daughter was an unforgettable day, as it is for most fathers, but my father didn't meet my sister until she was one year old. She was no longer a newborn baby but a young toddler. Her features and some of her mannerisms were pretty developed. Developed enough, that as my dad retells the story, he was faced with a princess that looked just like him. He was staring at his flesh and blood. It was nothing short of a sweet and memorable reunion.

My sister grew into a beautiful adolescent. She has resembled my father the most even after three more daughters were born. Throughout our childhood she remained very close to him. She was ever his helper, translating for him every time he ran errands. At the bank, the store, church. Everywhere. Not being able to speak English fluently put my father in need of a trustworthy translator. My sister became an extra-cautious and protective interpreter for him. She never wanted him to be mistreated or taken advantage of. She accurately interpreted every word for my father. No matter what, she was present and available to him. In the process, she taught her younger sisters to do the same as soon as we were old enough to help. From a very young age we learned what it meant to be responsible by helping out our family, by taking care of each other.

The stark resemblance between my father and sister was a funny thing—it definitely locked her identity to his, and not just genealogically—but genetically speaking it was evident he was in her DNA. She was Raul's daughter and everyone knew it, and she loved it.

When we think about Jesus, we see He came as the Son of God fully clothed in deity. He came fully clothed in the glory of God so that everyone would know He was God's Son.

We have gained the riches of His glory
from the fullness of His grace and truth.
A most precious inheritance delivered
directly into our hearts.

COME AND SEE

We have seen his glory, the glory of the one and only Son, who
came from the Father, full of grace and truth.
(JOHN 1:14B)

I imagine Jesus was present among His followers one day, when He heard stomachs growling and whispers of hunger. His disciples were not too keen on feeding the crowd. But Jesus was instantly moved to feed His people, to feed their starving bodies. Jesus received five loaves of bread and two fish from a young boy that day, and after thanking His Father for His provision, He multiplied the food and fed a crowd of more than 5,000 people. The Bible says that of all those present, not one went away hungry. And further still, there were twelve baskets full of leftover food.

Jesus came to Earth as a human being, yet He fully embodied God. Jesus came clothed in grace and truth and He came prepared to feed all of His followers. He had come with one purpose, to do the Father's will. In the heart of the Father His will was to claim the hearts of His people. He could neither act against His will nor His nature, and so met the need of the hungry that day. Upon performing this miracle, He remained with the crowd and He offered them an even better gift than food: a forever gift. Not just bread that would calm their aching stomachs for a few hours, but the Bread of Life that would calm their souls forever. He revealed to them that the daily bread they ate would not sustain them forever, but spiritual bread would. That forever bread is only available through Jesus. He is the Bread of Life. He is all that we need. So He fed their stomachs first, but then He fed their hungry souls. He gave them sustenance from His very creation and salvation from His very being (I encourage you to read the full story in John 6:1–15).

Much like my sister cannot change her features or the natural inclinations she inherited from her father, Jesus could not do or say anything that was in contradiction to His Father and His will.

> For I have not spoken on my own authority, but the Father who sent me has himself given me a commandment—what to say and what to speak.
> (John 12:49)

The disciples saw the Son—what a sight for sore eyes! They touched, heard, and saw their Savior. The disciples and Jesus' followers had the privilege of experiencing His glorious presence, miracles, healing power, wisdom, and holiness. They watched Jesus fully submit Himself to His Father's will and ultimately give His own life.

Through the testimony of the disciples through His Word, we are still able to see His glory. When we dig deeper into the miracles Jesus performed, we see the beauty in His submission, where physical provision and spiritual healing overlapped.

Dear Father,
Thank You that Your Word is a healing balm to my soul.
Thank You for being my provider, for feeding my soul which
longs for more and more of You. Help me to glorify You in
everything. In little and in much.
In Jesus' Name, Amen.

Reflect ~

Have you felt His healing power in your life? Have you seen His glory? If you haven't, ask God to reveal to you His grace and truth. Thank Him as you begin or continue to see His healing power in your life.

His Word ~

I pray that the eyes of your heart may be enlightened in order that you may know the hope to which he has called you, the riches of his glorious inheritance in his holy people. (Ephesians 1:18)

~ *Nine* ~

JESUS IS ALWAYS THE GOOD NEWS

THE ILLNESS CAME ON suddenly and overwhelmed me. It interrupted my husband's, my daughters', and my life as we knew it. Nothing could have prepared us for this. No longer able to leave the house, take my daughters to school, walk outside or feed myself, I was temporarily incapacitated. What I could have never expected was how quickly it would transform my life. No sooner had I been on a family camping trip then I was lying in bed for hours on end. And my, was it a wake-up call.

Over the course of being bedridden for five months, I became devoted to reading all that I could take in from His Word. Authors like Francis Chan in *Crazy Love* helped me fall in love with my Maker. Books like *Knowing God,* by J. I. Packer, taught me who my God really is. And so I realized, it wasn't only about *remaining* on the right path, it was about helping others *find* the right path. I had been invited to share in the Good News of Jesus from a very young age. My parents had taught me His truths at home, but I was keeping this amazing gift all to myself and I wasn't sharing it with friends and family who also desperately needed to hear about hope in Him.

I thought I had been living with purpose and intention. I was raising my girls to love and honor Jesus. I thought that finding a church and attending weekly Bible Study was all I had to do to stay on the right path. These things in and of themselves were honorable, but there was more to life than remaining on the right path.

In reality, I had become a luke-warm, comfort-seeking Christian who needed to grow and know her Creator. I mean *really* know Him.

Though five years later I continue to struggle—sometimes on a daily basis—with sickness and pain, I have never felt more purpose in my life. I realize this is so often the point of our trials—to have everything pulled out from under you so that all that is left is you and Jesus—because it is just as much about the journey as it is about the destination. You have to go through the wilderness to get to the promised land. I would not be who I am today had I not gone through my own wilderness. So we don't have to fear adversity, obstacles, or trials. There is great purpose in them. Without them, I would not have learned that what God desires from my life is my whole heart. There are too many hurting hearts in this world. I can no longer keep His promises and truths to myself.

Jesus is always the Good News.

COME AND SEE

John testified concerning him. He cried out, saying, "This is the one I spoke about when I said, 'He who comes after me has surpassed me because he was before me.'"
(JOHN 1:15)

Don't you love to receive good news? Like the kind that is sprung on you when you least expect it and puts a smile on your face that no one can wipe off? I believe this is exactly how John the Baptist responds to his calling, to his knowing about the Good News of Jesus. He wants to share it with the world and it's such a strong force that no one can stop him.

John the Baptist is sent out by God to announce that the King is coming. He is announcing the Good Message like a farmer spreading seeds on fertile soil in anticipation of a plentiful harvest. I believe John the Baptist anticipated hearts rejoicing at the news of Jesus' arrival. Now, the time had come for Jesus to present Himself as the Son of God, to leave His home with Mary and Joseph and go out and preach the truth of who He was, the truth of who sent Him and where He was going. So with great power and celebration, John the Baptist points to Jesus and shouts that this is the man, the Messiah, he had been proclaiming all along. He cried out to all those around him so that they would turn to him and listen, that they might turn their lives around and walk toward Jesus.

John the Baptist announces the fulfillment of the most profound prophecy in history: the long-awaited King entering our world to be given as a ransom for us all. He wants all to see the manifestation of the Son before their very eyes. What was prophesied is coming to pass and I imagine he wants to yell from the top of his lungs, "*Come* and *See* the MESSIAH!"

So he cried out and pointed everyone to Jesus and His eternal life. I'm overwhelmed with joy by the thought of being handed down this great kingdom work. I'm challenged in my most difficult days and trials, to dare to cry out and point those around me to Jesus. Maybe this is the point of it all, to testify in the heart of our suffering to The One who was, who is, and who will always be. Though I have not seen full physical healing from my illness, my broken body given for His sake meets His healing hand and that makes me whole. In this wholeness, I'm encouraged to, like John the Baptist, spread the Good News!

May we all point to the One who through our darkest days leads us through green pastures and makes us whole (Psalm 23).

Dear Father,
Thank You that You are revealing to me the Good News of
Your salvation. Thank You that Your saving grace is eternal
and the greatest gift to my life. Help me to always remember
that You are with me, that You are in me, and that You are for
me. You are the Good News every day!
In Jesus' Name, Amen.

Reflect ~

Have you understood the Good News of Jesus Christ? If you have, believe and receive Him today. Find a quiet space where you can talk to Jesus. A special prayer called "Decision Prayer" has been written at the end of this book to help guide you. If you haven't understood the Good News, I encourage you to read the entire book of John in the Bible. And I pray that by also reading *Come and See*, you will fully understand, by the end of the book, that Jesus is the Good News and that He calls you into His heart to love and receive His gift of life, forever.

His Word ~

The people walking in darkness have seen a great light; on those living in the land of deep darkness a light has dawned. (Isaiah 9:2)

~ *Ten* ~

"AM I WILLING TO GIVE ALL THAT I HAVE TO HIM?"

HE SAT QUIETLY, RESERVED, on a small stool with a money dish placed before him, and yet his presence demanded my attention. Thin and fragile, with sparkly, light hazel eyes, his look so deep, so profound, radiating an inexplicable light. That he was a Spaniard is all I knew of him, yet I couldn't shake off the feeling as I walked past him that I was supposed to go back. I continued walking through the Plaza Mayor there in Madrid, my husband and I searching for a place to have lunch. Still thinking about him through lunch and into dessert, I thought "How can I enjoy this meal while this man sits there hungry and starved?" I prayed, "Oh Jesus, may I be brave enough to feed him." It was obvious he needed a meal or two, so after lunch I returned to him with food in hand. I knelt and looked him in the eye, "Can I offer you some lunch?" Our eyes locked; his were so sweet, so loving. He reached up and excitedly replied, "Yes." I handed him the bag of food and placed my hand on his shoulder, and I told him without even hesitating or remembering that I was talking to a complete stranger, "You are so sweet and precious." And he responded, "So are you." My heart melted. I didn't want to leave his presence. Why wasn't there a stool or a chair nearby I could pull up to sit with him? I smiled and stayed a while, just staring. But then it was time to walk away. I continued looking back at him, tears beginning to trickle down my face. But why?

This story has remained with me since my trip. As I meditated and thought about that day, those eyes, that gentle and sweet spirit, it occurred to me that this was three days before I would enter a very dark time where I would face fear like I've never known, and pain like I've never felt. Yet Jesus would visit me on that day. It was his eyes that reminded me of His fullness, His grace, His compassion. Did Jesus not say, "Do not forget to show hospitality to strangers, for by so doing some people have shown hospitality to angels without knowing it" (Hebrews 13:2)? Was he an angel? He most certainly was sent to comfort me and touch my heart. How is it that in appearance this gentleman was a beggar in need of a meal, and yet he gave me so much more than I could have given him? He was not a beggar, but a giver. He reminded me of my father back at home and that felt so reassuring, endearing, so lovely and so familiar. And so I realized it was my Father in heaven who was looking upon me. It was my Jesus giving me grace in place of grace from His fullness. His Spirit in mine, going ahead of me to prepare me for a trial where one dreadful night, far from home, my husband would cradle me and bathe me like a baby as I trembled, ached, and cried. Wanting to come home, I was more than 5,000 miles away, three days from departure, and three flights from home.

God's presence through this lovely Spaniard would comfort and console me, and it would remind me that He is always with us. He does not sleep or slumber, and His grace is always upon us. I made it home safely on that trip because He carried me home.

And it makes me realize, Jesus loved all and gave Himself wholly. I'm challenged to ask: Am I not to do the same?

"Am I willing to give all that I have to Him?
And God forbid -
what if He hadn't given me all that He is?[1]

---

1. Voskamp, *Broken Way*, 47.

COME AND SEE

*Out of his fullness we have all received grace
in place of grace already given.*
(JOHN 1:16)

Have you ever found yourself in a situation where you have not received the benefit of the doubt? Where someone has chosen to believe the worst in you, instead of the best? I have been on the receiving end and the giving end of this scenario, where I have chosen doubt instead of belief in someone else. In a way, I believe that this verse exemplifies this in a most profound way. The apostle John is explaining to us here that we are the recipients of Jesus' grace. We have received His grace even without knowing it, even without asking for it. Jesus came to save us from an eternity in hell. From the beginning Jesus wanted us to chose Him. Because there is a choice to make. When we believe in Him, we receive more of His grace, we become His children, just as He promised. So it's eternal life over mortal life and a continuation of His grace throughout our lives.

> "Just as a careful gardener will stand over a plant that needs water, and will pour the water on the surface until the earth has drunk it up, and then add a little more; so He gives step by step, grace for grace, an uninterrupted bestowal, yet regulated according to the absorbing power of the heart that receives it. Underlying that great thought are two things: the continuous communication of grace, and the progressive communication of grace. We have here the continuous communication of grace. God is always pouring Himself out upon us in Christ. There is a perpetual out flow from Him to us: if there is not a perpetual inflow into us from Him it is our fault, and not His. He is always giving, and His intention is that our lives shall be a continual reception."[2]

He was sent to us. Then His life was given for us—all of Him for all of us. His fullness (nothing being spared). And it didn't end

2. MacLaren, "John 1:16," para. 2.

there. He conquered death and came back to life, His favor upon us every step of the way. Because out of His fullness we receive overflowing grace, we are showered with favor after favor—grace upon grace—more of Him. The more we seek, the more we find. The more we hunger, the more we are fed.

Dear Father,
Thank You for sparing nothing. Help me to give out of Your fullness, to a hurting world. Give me the eyes to see those who are in pain. May Your Spirit in me bring them peace and comfort.
In Jesus' Name, Amen.

Reflect ~

Have you given all that you are to Him? Meditate on this and ask Jesus to help you give all that you have, and all that you are, to Him.

His Word ~

He must become greater; I must become less. (John 3:30)

~ Eleven ~

HIS GRACE AND TRUTH
ARE FAR SUPERIOR

THERE IS A BEAUTIFUL story further on in the book of John, in chapter 8, verses 3 through 11, that I want to share with you. I believe there is no better story for me to share with you today that symbolizes God's outspoken redemptive love. The story begins with a group of religious men, the religious elite, questioning Jesus about the consequences a woman should face for committing adultery. The men press Jesus for an answer. To their surprise, Jesus does not condemn her, instead He frees her. His sweet gift of grace.

Jesus was presented with a rather straightforward case, or so the accusers thought. Prepping for her capital punishment for committing adultery, the men brought her to Jesus. There she was, in The LORD's presence. I imagine she was mistreated. Thrown to the ground, hated, and embarrassed, was she on her knees, covering her head and face as she awaited the first stone to hit her? Jesus met her right there, right in that place of humiliation. He stooped down to her level and wrote in the dust, the very dust by which He created mankind. The very dust our bodies came from and in which we will end up after we die. Our bodies start and end in dust: "For dust you are and to dust you will return" (Genesis 3:19). Yet that day, the day she met her Maker, she would not meet death, she would meet life. Jesus said so much through His silence when He knelt down and wrote in the dust. In this way He said, "I am with you, I am right here. I am for you, not against you. I came to save you, not harm you." Jesus demonstrated His servant's heart in His kneeling and stooping down, just like He would do when He washed the disciples' feet later on (John 13:1–17).

Down at her level, He wrote with the very finger He drew man with, where all of humanity began. While the religious elite pressed to end her life, He pressed in to save her life. It's a humbling reflection to think that while they accused her of her sin in public, the great I AM vindicated her of her sin personally, yet publicly. Nothing is too low that His love cannot forgive. And He humbled the religious people by demonstrating that His love heals all sins of all sinners. How often do we feel superior to others because they sin differently than we do? But Jesus didn't condemn her. He met her where she was and set her free.

He not only set her free, He also set the accusers free that day. Free to not live under judgment of others. Free to see others in light of their Creator and not their sin. Jesus stooped down twice. John 8:9b says "Only Jesus was left in the middle of the crowd with the woman." When He shows up, only you and He are left. He fights your battles and your accuser departs. Satan is the father of lies and your greatest accuser. Yet Jesus shows up to defend you and to set you free!

> Then Jesus stood up again and said to the woman, "Where are your accusers? Didn't even one of them condemn you?"
>
> "No, Lord," she said.
>
> And Jesus said, "Neither do I. Go and sin no more." (John 8:10–11)

Over and over we see how Jesus deals with us in the same manner He dealt with the humbled woman: in grace He offers her no condemnation but in truth He says go and sin no more.

His grace and truth are far surperior
to anyone's accusations.
His is absolute truth bestowed upon us
in the greatest love story there ever was.

COME AND SEE

For the law was given through Moses;
grace and truth came through Jesus Christ.
(JOHN 1:17)

I can think of a time when I was younger and preferred to hear the advice of another parent over my own parents' advice. I admired my friend's parents, and so I suppose I respected their advice slightly more. I'm so embarrassed to say these things now. My parents only wanted the best for me, yet somehow I couldn't see it back then. In a way, I think this is how the Jews felt about Moses. They had learned about him since birth and they knew Moses as their spiritual leader who had come to bless their entire nation. There was no doubt he had been a man of God, and yet they could not see that Jesus, no doubt the Son of God, had come as their holy and just Savior. So Moses was more important to them. He was admired and respected. And Jesus came not to take any of that away from them, but He came to fulfill the law that had been given through Moses. And even more, He came to give His grace (unfailing love) and truth (that we are sinners) to all who would accept it. Through it He would usher in a new promise, a new covenant for the world.

Moses was used to deliver the law to the people of Israel; the Levitical law as it was called. The law specified many things, including the Ten Commandments, offerings and sacrifices to God, building God's temple (called the tabernacle), and the role of the priesthood. So Moses played an important and powerful role in delivering the law. For this, the Israelites held him in very high esteem. It is in this light that the apostle John sees the need to clarify that, though the holy and righteous law was given through Moses, at the will of the Father, grace and truth came through Jesus Christ, also at the will of the Father. Their salvation would now come through the perfect and blameless Messiah. He had entered the world with a new promise, a new order under the era of grace.

> That is why he is the one who mediates a new covenant between God and people, so that all who are called can receive the eternal inheritance God has promised them. For Christ died to set them free from the penalty of the sins they had committed under that first covenant. (Hebrews 9:15)

So while the law was given through Moses, a prophet and holy man in the eyes of God, the eternal and life-giving gifts of grace and truth came through Jesus Christ, the Righteous One. Jesus was the only One who could fulfill the law perfectly because He is holy, blameless and sinless. In fulfilling the law, He removed the power of sin over our lives.

Dear Father,
Thank You for seeing me and not accusing me. Thank You for always forgiving me. Help me, Jesus. Help me to give someone else Your grace and truth instead of the devil's hate and lies. May I be reminded that I live under a new promise that reveals Your love in me, that I may spread Your love to others. In Jesus' Name, Amen.

Reflect ~

Does the story of the adulterous woman resonate with you? How so? Meditate on this and thank Jesus that He remakes the adulterous woman into the loved woman that she is. He does the same for you and me.

His Word ~

For God so loved the world that he gave his one and only Son, that whoever believes in him shall not perish but have eternal life. For God did not send his Son into the world to condemn the world, but to save the world through him. (John 3:16–17)

~ Twelve ~

HIS LOVE SO PROFOUND

As an official junior in High School, I prepared to visit Guatemala that summer and complete a month of missions work at a local orphanage there. I was excited to travel independent of my parents at the age of fifteen! I would travel with high school friends and I'd meet new friends from all over the US. Summer could not come fast enough!

When my month was up, I would not fly home with the rest of the group. Instead, I chose to extend my trip and stay with my sister who was completing a teaching program in the city's capitol, while living with my *abuelita Cristy* (grandmother). So I tagged along and visited my sister's school for four extra weeks. I became quite close to the teachers at the school as I spent most of my days in the teacher's lounge while she taught. I thought "I could just stay and live here forever." I absolutely loved it.

It wasn't until I woke up one day to some very painful cramping and bleeding, that I wanted to go home. I felt excessive pain and weakness. At the age of fifteen, what was I to know but lay in bed and rest? Not drinking enough water or eating enough because of my loss of appetite, I became weaker and weaker by the minute. The hemorrhaging increased with each passing day.

My aunt, who was like a second mother to me, was visiting Guatemala that summer as well. Upon learning the news, she showed up at my grandmother's doorstep. She saw firsthand the horror that I was living. Unable to pull myself out of bed, I would fall to the floor and crawl to the bathroom feeling dizzier and dizzier by the minute. My heart pounding, my head aching, my vision distorted, I would barely make it back into bed.

It was late one night when my aunt decided to take me back to the house she was staying at to watch over me. She scrambled to find a doctor who could see me. Family members jumped in to help us. I remember lying in bed that night, unable to sleep because the sound of my beating heart against the mattrees was so loud and pronounced. My poor heart was working overtime.

Upon arriving at the clinic, we were told that my hemoglobin count had dropped to three. I would not have made it another night had my aunt not intervened along with other family members. It would be the love of my late uncle that would take him through the streets, from bus to bus, blood bank to blood bank, to find my blood type. It was in this tiny, makeshift clinic, out of the house of a doctor, that I would receive care and a life-saving blood transfusion. My first taste of a near-death experience, 3,000 miles away from my *mami* and *papi*. My sister and aunt at my bedside, prayed and cried and prayed some more. My Savior rescued me at my bedside and reminded me that His blood was given for mine and that I would live for all eternity. His love wrapped me in layers and layers of family, friends, blood donors (my sweet uncle being one of them), and teachers and staff from my sister's school.

My Jesus saved me and healed me that night. How is it that when we reach unimaginable lows in life, we see Him best? He surrounds us with loving and selfless people, even strangers. As Isaiah the prophet was humbled before God at the gravity of his own mortal existence, I was humbled at the existence of my weakness and my very mortal need for a majestic healing power, a supernatural power that could only come from my Father above. To feel His presence, His love, His resurrection, and the power of His blood overwhelms me and causes unspeakable joy.

His love so profound
He not sparing anything or anyOne
bestowed on us Himself.

COME AND SEE

No one has ever seen God, but the one and only Son, who is himself God and is in closest relationship with the Father, has made him known.
(JOHN 1:18)

Jesus has come to make His Father known to us. King Jesus was presented to us in holy flesh and blood on Christmas morning. He came that He might make the mystery of His Father, the works of His Father, the plans of His Father, and most importantly, the love of His Father, known to us. He preached to the multitudes and He invited us all in to share in the knowledge and pleasure of the Father. We know the Father when we know Jesus.

> The Son is the radiance of God's glory and the exact representation of his being, sustaining all things by his powerful word. After he had provided purification for sins, he sat down at the right hand of the Majesty in heaven. (Hebrews 1:3)

The prophet Isaiah describes a time when he saw a vision of God and the very emotion and fear that overtook him. The temple was filled with light and holiness. Holiness that demanded he bow down and repent to Him. Light that demanded he bow down and praise Him. Light that was so pure that Isaiah's sin surfaced and he thought he would die. The contrast between holiness and sin is so profound.

> In the year that King Uzziah died, I saw the Lord, high and exalted, seated on a throne; and the train of his robe filled the temple. Above him were seraphim, each with six wings: With two wings they covered their faces, with two they covered their feet, and with two they were flying. And they were calling to one another:
>
>> "Holy, holy, holy is the LORD Almighty;
>> the whole earth is full of his glory."
>
> At the sound of their voices the doorposts and thresholds shook and the temple was filled with smoke.

"Woe to me!" I cried. "I am ruined! For I am a man
of unclean lips, and I live among a people of unclean lips,
and my eyes have seen the King, the LORD Almighty."
(Isaiah 6:1–6)

Seeing Him in a vision, Isaiah could not even catch a glimpse of
God—His presence was too holy a sight. So The Father sent His
Son as the very representation of God's being, that through Jesus
we might see Him, and through seeing, we might believe in God
who is wise, sovereign, loving, truthful, gracious, merciful, holy,
and divine. What love the Father has for His children that He
would send His only Son, who is at His side eternally, to demon-
strate to us how far He would go to show us how "wide and long
and high and deep is the love of Christ" (Ephesians 3:18).

Dear Father,
Thank You for sending Your Son to shed His blood so that I
could be saved from eternal death. Your power overwhelms
me as Your love embraces me. I want to honor You every day
of my life. Help me to remember each and every day that You
stopped at nothing, spared nothing, to save me. I love you,
Lord.
In Jesus' Name, Amen.

Reflect ~

Have you ever thought about what it means to you personally that
God sent His only and sinless Son to die? Meditate on this. Let your
heart fill with joy and gratitude at the thought of His love for you.

His Word ~

After Jesus said this, he looked toward heaven and prayed:

"Father, the hour has come. Glorify your Son, that your Son may glorify you. For you granted him authority over all people that he might give eternal life to all those you have given him." (John 17:1–2)

~ *Thirteen* ~

PRAISE HIM THAT OUR EVER-CHANGING WORLD WILL NEVER CHANGE HIM

THE MORNING ALARM THE following day was the subtle sounds of little hands on a keyboard. My daughter, wide awake, staring at the computer at 6:30 a.m. How long had she been there? She had woken up at 6 a.m. and dashed over to the desk to find the results online. I saw her and immediately reached in to hug her and assure her that no matter what, everything would be okay, though I myself needed to hear these words. She looked up, uncertainty in her eyes, not really knowing what it all meant; yet her eyes were so innocent, so bright, so full of life.

The beauty that rises above uncertainty is always Jesus. His life brightens our days and lights the way for our future. How often I become entangled with current events or exasperated by the present realities and the future unknowns.

A very sober reminder of this came during this last election in the US, with emotions and worry dominating our lives for the months leading up to the election. My sweet girls, husband, and I watched the results with trepidation on the evening of November 8. The colors red and blue popped up from coast to coast, and my eldest daughter tried to keep up by coloring in her printout of the United States. At the end of the night we had to insist that we all go to bed and rest up after a day filled with unknowns and anxiety.

We had to remind ourselves that our hope rested in the LORD and not in the results.

But if this was true, then why had I made more of this election than I should have? I worried for my daughters' future. I worried about what it meant for our day-to-day life. Yet even today, I find Jesus reminding me that He did not come to win an election. He did not come to save the Jewish nation from a ruling power. He came to save us from a life of eternal darkness. And that is the point of it all. We should be the light to this world, we should share this gift with others. And no matter how difficult and oppressive things may become, we should not be silent. We are to spread love through our healing words, His Word, feeding the hungry, clothing the poor, encouraging the persecuted, helping the enslaved, rescuing the exploited, fighting for the victimized, and listening and praying for the bullied among a great many other things. We are to be a mobile hospital, a place of refuge everywhere we go to point everyone to Jesus. So our hope is not in any one, in any thing, or in any group here on Earth. Our hope is fully in the Lord!

Moral compasses will sway, political views will resound, but His truth and His light will never change. His light is always light. His power never diminishes nor do His truths ever change.

Praise Him that our ever-changing world
will never change Him.

COME AND SEE

Now this was John's testimony when the Jewish leaders in Jerusalem sent priests and Levites to ask him who he was. He did not fail to confess, but confessed freely, "I am not the Messiah."
They asked him, "Then who are you? Are you Elijah?"
He said, "I am not."
"Are you the Prophet?"
He answered, "No."
(JOHN 1:19–21)

Who are you? I suspect this is a question you have been asked more than once in your life, and I imagine you have answered, "I am . . ." and then stated either your name or maybe your profession. When asked this same question, John the Baptist does not answer in a way we would expect with an "I am" statement. Instead, his words are: "I AM NOT." John humbly and graciously confesses he is not Jesus Christ. Not wanting to confuse or mislead, he boldly states the truth. In contrast to Jesus' response in John 8:58—"'Very truly I tell you,' Jesus answered, 'before Abraham was born, I am!'"— John's confession is, "I am not." As Matthew Henry puts it: "His disowning himself to be the Christ is called his confessing and not denying Christ."[1]

For the previous 400 years, the people of Israel had not had a prophet to lead them or counsel them as had been the case in the previous centuries. So they awaited their Messiah, their Christ, their Prophet who would bring them hope in an era of Roman rule. But John the Baptist emphatically stated that he was not the Christ. So they asked him if he was Elijah. And he stated, yet again, that he was not.

If we look back at the story of Elijah the prophet and his ascension to heaven, we are reminded that he did not die a natural death. He literally ascended. He was taken into heaven in a whirlwind with chariots of fire (I encourage you to read this jaw-dropping story in 2 Kings 2). The religious leaders may have wondered if Elijah had come back since he never actually died. John the Baptist sets the record straight by saying he is neither Elijah, nor the Prophet they awaited.

How easy it would have been for John the Baptist to run with this new narrative that he was the prophet, and to take on a new identity, albeit a false one. But he remained faithful to Jesus till the end. A vessel for God's kingdom, He baptized with water and spread the message that Jesus was coming. His message was one of hope and truth, something the Israelites longed for after a long period of silence.

1. Henry, "John 1:19," III. 1. (1). [1.].

The Jews anticipated their Savior who would release them from Roman rule. They were tired of being ruled by the opposition and they wanted to be freed and left alone to practice Jewish law. So the Jewish leaders were filled with hope and excitement when they learned of John the Baptist. So much so, that when John the Baptist confirmed he was not the Messiah, they became uncomfortable. They wanted him to be someone of significant value and worth. Someone who would have all the answers, who would rescue them from their personal and political turmoil. They didn't want to hear the truth. If they had stopped to listen in that moment, they would have heard John proclaiming the King was coming, that their Savior was just days away from them.

It's easy to miss Jesus through it all. Those who didn't understand who John the Baptist was were more preoccupied with making him someone he was not. They failed to hear the true message of the Gospel. May we not repeat the same mistake.

Dear Father,
Thank You that You are always ready to quiet my anxious inclination. I so often get carried away with all the white noise that I forget to let You quiet my soul so I can hear Your voice. Help me to see You in all aspects of my life, as hopeless as they may seem. Help me to remember that You are my helper. In Jesus' Name, Amen.

Reflect ~

What worries you today? Meditate on His promise that "If God is for us, who can be against us" (Romans 8:31b)? Tell him your worries and then quietly wait for His peace.

His Word ~

So do not fear, for I am with you;
do not be dismayed, for I am your God.
I will strengthen you and help you;
I will uphold you with my righteous right hand. (Isaiah 41:10)

~ *Fourteen* ~

LET HIM ENTER YOUR WILDERNESS

WRITING THIS BOOK WAS incredibly difficult in and of itself, and sometimes outside circumstances seemed to be conspiring against me. There were days when the spiritual battle was so intense. I suppose it has given me more stories to share with you! Last year, as I began spending more of my days in writing, I found myself in one of the busiest seasons of my life. Too many things were happening all at once. My husband started traveling more and one of my daughter's activities increased significantly. I had dedicated my time to raising my girls and taking care of our home the last eight years. In this new school year, however, I would enter a new and exciting season. With a book deal in place, I would be writing all day long, or so I hoped. It always amazes me how few hours there are in a day.

It all came to a grinding halt when one night, while my husband was traveling, Chewie (our sweet pup) and I heard a noise in the family room. Before I could even react to the noise, Chewie started growling. I wanted him to be quiet, to not wake up the girls. But there it was again, a rattling noise followed by scratching. I immediately jumped out of my bed and then slowly tiptoed into the kitchen. I turned on the light and then reached into the family room to turn the switch on as fast as I could. I stared into the room to see if I could find anything out of place or maybe see the door knob rotate. To be honest, I'm not sure what my next move would have been if I had seen the door knob rotate, but that was not what happened. As I stood there staring into the room, all of a sudden I saw a large, disgusting rat, just sitting there. It was frozen by that point, just as I was. Neither of us knew what to do. Startled by each other's presence, I screamed. But it wasn't like a normal scream that comes out of your mouth; this was an internalized, I'm-so-scared-and-grossed-out kind of inner scream that reverberated throughout my body. I 100 percent freaked out. I'd love to say I went in there and killed it and handled it like a boss. But I didn't. I pretty much did not sleep that entire night just thinking about it, and soon I became so upset because the family room was where I had been writing for days. My laptop sat on the couch just above where the stinky rat had been. I had found the perfect spot to write and now I couldn't bear being in the same room as a rodent.

I'd love to say that my interruptions while writing ended there. But a few weeks later, as the family left for work and school, I found a new spot to write in: my kitchen. I embraced it and enjoyed my new, sunnier space. Well, one morning I was sitting there writing when all of a sudden I heard water gushing from below me. I could hear it, but I couldn't see it. What is it with me chasing noises? Before I could chase the sound any further, I saw my kitchen begin to flood. Water was gushing onto my kitchen floor from beneath the sink. I opened the cabinet doors to hot steam and a powerful stream of water. I couldn't seem to find the valve fast enough to turn off the water, so I instinctively turned off the dishwasher and that did the trick. But then I was left with this huge puddle in my kitchen. It turns out the pipe had become unscrewed, causing the water to leak into the cabinet. Thank God I was able to fix it, clean it up, and go back to writing, but I lost precious hours of writing time, not to mention concentration.

And that wasn't the end of it. But I'll save that for another day! Distractions and interruptions abound, and the enemy works hard to unsettle us, and so our best move is inviting Jesus into our interruptions, even more, our wilderness. From the wilderness came the most powerful voice calling us to make our path straight for Jesus.

Let Him enter your wilderness,
Let Him save you.

COME AND SEE

Finally they said, "Who are you? Give us an answer to take back
to those who sent us. What do you say about yourself?"
John replied in the words of Isaiah the prophet, "I am the voice of
one calling in the wilderness, 'Make straight the way for the Lord.'"
(JOHN 1:22–23)

Again, they asked him, "Who are you?" Only this time, I believe they were ready to hear the answer. I'm not sure they were going to like the answer, but they sure were curious and eager to hear John the Baptist's response. And he replied, not with his own words, but with an Old Testament prophecy: "I am the voice of one calling in the wilderness, 'Make straight the way for the Lord'" (Isaiah 40:3). This would certainly have gotten their attention. Jewish leaders would have recognized this quote from their study of Isaiah and they would hopefully have made the connection and celebrated the fact that their Messiah was coming.

When Isaiah spoke these same words hundreds of years earlier, they were words of comfort for the Jews. They had been banned from their land while under Babylonian rule. Isaiah was announcing that their return to their land was imminent, so these words were of immense consolation. Isaiah was telling them that their kingdom would soon be restored. You can imagine how wonderful it must have felt to receive this good news, to hear that they would be returning home soon. But of even more importance, in these specific verses, Isaiah was pointing to a far more important event. He foretells that a voice in the wilderness, in the desert, would come shouting that all should prepare a path for Jesus to enter. He was calling people to repentance that would lead to obedience for the reconciliation of their sin.

John the Baptist referred back to that verse in Isaiah about the prophecy being fulfilled, and this time, not under Babylonian rule, but under Roman order. The Jews waited for their salvation from the Romans, except this time, they would not be freed in the political sense. No, because Jesus didn't come to secure a political future for Israel. He came to secure an eternal home for us all in heaven, to be in His presence forever. So the shackles of sin and religion would be removed to usher in a life of spiritual liberty. Jesus was here to bring them eternal salvation from hell. But would they receive Him? Would they let Him enter their wilderness?

> "When eastern princes marched through desert countries, ways were prepared for them, and hinderances removed. And may the Lord prepare our hearts by the teaching of his word and the convictions of his Spirit, that high and proud thoughts may be brought down, good desires planted, crooked and rugged tempers made straight and softened, and every hinderance removed, that we may be ready for his will on earth, and prepared for his heavenly kingdom."[1]

Dear Father,
Thank You that You are my helper and my defender. Save me from the wilderness I am facing today. I need Your grace. Help me to look up and call on Your name.
In Jesus' Name, Amen.

Reflect ~

Do you find yourself in the wilderness today? Allow God to be your helper and defender. Talk to Him and let Him lead You into His arms where you are safe.

1. Henry, "Isaiah 40:1," para. 1.

His Word ~

Come with great power, O God, and rescue me! Defend me with
your might. (Psalm 54:1 NLT)

~ *Fifteen* ~

WHEN YOU'RE SO FOCUSED ON DOING RIGHT, YOU LOSE SIGHT

I TRULY LOVED MY childhood home church. It was a place where I was known and loved. I especially loved hearing Bible stories. And it was all because of a sweet teacher I will never forget: Mrs. Potter. She made stories come to life. They were vivid depictions, full of life and color. She told Bible stories through very vibrant illustrations printed on large stock paper. She transported every listener to the setting of the story and it was as if you could see, smell, hear, touch, and taste the story, scene after scene. To this day, I get that same childhood excitement when I read a Bible story, thanks to her.

But despite learning these amazing and important stories as a young child, things began to shift in my church as I got older. The teaching became less about Jesus and more about my behavior, the way I dressed, the language I used, and a list of do's and don'ts. It became more about memorizing the order of the books of the Bible, and less about the message and the stories that filled those pages. It quite honestly became boring and monotonous, and the true essence of Jesus was lost.

As I reflect many years later, I think about what brought me back to the church after walking away for a time, like some of the children that I grew up with. It is those same stories I learned as a young child that would lead me right back into my Father's arms. Because you see, the part that was lost in religion those later years was the love and mercy of Jesus. So when you return to His Word, you read and fall in love with the Author, again and again. That same excitement, that seed that was planted as a child, blossoms because you've found the true essence of the Bible: Jesus! And then you naturally want to serve Him and honor Him with your life.

So those unnecessary and destructive rules and regulations don't get to control or torment you anymore. You are no longer judged, but justified, and His mercy just envelops you. You learn that He took on the punishment you deserve so that you don't have to be judged or condemned. So in reality, you're no longer captive to rules and regulations; you're free to live a holy and justified life because of Him. All of a sudden, it becomes less about you, and more about Him, so those behaviors the church tried to drill into you, the ones you ran from, naturally occur as you serve Jesus, as the Holy Spirit produces the fruit of love, faithfulness, and self-control in you.

When you're so focused on doing right,
you lose sight of who you're doing it for.
Focus intently on Jesus and doing right will follow.

COME AND SEE

Now the Pharisees who had been sent questioned him, "Why then do you baptize if you are not the Messiah, nor Elijah, nor the Prophet?"
(JOHN 1:24–25)

Not hearing what they had hoped to hear, the Pharisees, confused and intrigued, asked John the Baptist this final question: "Why then . . .?" If he in fact was not the long-awaited Savior, then who had given him the authority to baptize? Certainly, the Pharisees, being experts of the law, had been educated and had earned this title. Yet this John came out of nowhere (literally out of the wilderness) with a message so profound, and he even had disciples, men he was leading on this crusade for Jesus. I'm sure they thought that the Messiah would be revealed to them first, and so I think it's safe to say that John the Baptist posed a serious threat to the Jewish leaders.

What the Pharisees failed to understand, however, was one important thing: when God calls you to serve and to minister to others, He gives you the platform you need to get His message out. His message, through His Spirit, is put in you so that you can then sing it out to those who need to hear it. He gives you the authority to speak. He gives you the schooling. His crucified hands pass His message along to you, that you might then pass along His blessing to others. Hand to hand. Heart to heart. A high calling from the High King.

"Why then?" they asked. But what they really meant was, "How dare you?" They too could have accepted His message and high calling on their lives, but instead the Pharisees chose to resist Him. They were too blind to see that this gift was for them too. Jesus was calling the high and mighty and the low and unmighty, because you see, the gospel is for *everyone*. But sometimes the high and mighty are so high up on their pedestals, they miss out on what's happening down below. The true miracle is happening below them, but they're too proud to see it, so they quite literally *over*see it from above because otherwise they'd have to stare it straight in the eye. But it's much easier to keep on living your current life. Your current, comfortable, blind life. Opening up to the truth is not easy because it challenges your status quo. So they just kept on keeping on.

The Pharisees were leaders in their own right, but they had deviated from God's Word. Over time, they had added to the Word of God and followed tradition religiously and lost sight of the true essence and teachings of God. This is the main reason they failed to see Jesus when He arrived. They gave equal, if not more, authority to a list of traditions and ways than they did to His written and spoken Word. In it, they would have seen that Jesus fulfilled the prophecies laid out for them in the Old Testament books. Instead, they partnered with the opposing political party, the Sadducees, and together they convicted Jesus. Neither had eyes to see Him.

So the best I can summarize it is like this: let us not follow a legalistic way of life, following traditions over Scripture and obeying a set of rules and rituals over Scripture. Because, my God, if we do this, we then miss You altogether.

Dear Father,
Forgive me for taking my focus off of You. Thank You so much
for Your Word that reminds me of the truth of who You are.
Help me to keep my eyes on You all the days of my life. When
the voices of judgment and criticism come my way, help me to
have the strength to turn them over to You.
In Jesus' Name, Amen.

Reflect ~

Has the legalism of religion discouraged you? I'm so sorry. Today, lay this all out at the feet of Jesus and ask Him to show you who He really is.

His Word ~

For it is by grace you have been saved, through faith—and this is not from yourselves, it is the gift of God—not by works, so that no one can boast. (Ephesians 2:8–9)

~ *Sixteen* ~

MAY THE ATTENTION WE ONCE ENJOYED FROM OTHERS PALE IN COMPARISON

GETTING ATTENTION HAS ALWAYS seemed attractive to me. As the third-born daughter of four, I always enjoyed getting attention over my other sisters. I suppose it didn't help that I was the youngest for seven years until my younger sister was born. I became accustomed to the endearing nicknames like *Chispita* (spark). I liked knowing that everyone found me cute and that I could be a spark of joy for the family.

But sometimes good things come to an end. Seemingly good things, that is. Because when my younger sister was born, the attention definitely lessened. This sweet little girl had won the hearts of all those who held her. Even I became fully consumed with the baby in my arms. I loved rocking her to sleep while my mom cooked. She was my new baby doll and the best part is she was a real-life American Girl. With her big, dark brown eyes, long black eyelashes, shiny hair, rosy cheeks and pink lips, she was beautiful.

Sharing the attention took some getting used to at first. It's a good thing she was so darn cute! In a way, it was like I had exchanged all the attention from others for the attention of one cute, little person. And that was all worth it. When she cried, I ran to console her. When she woke up from her nap I crawled into her crib to play. When she got hungry, I gave her a warm bottle. I read her books and I cradled her. Every day was a playdate and I loved getting her attention.

I wonder if this is what it looks like when we decide to live for Jesus. The attention we enjoyed from others pales in comparison to the love and compassion we receive from Jesus. The words we read in the pages of the Bible jump out at us and become so real and personal. There are days it feels like the verses were written specifically for me, specifically for my situation at that very moment. Jesus becomes so personal. All of His attention for all of ours.

May the attention we once enjoyed from others
pale in comparison to the joy of having
all of His attention.

COME AND SEE

"I baptize with water," John replied, "but among you stands
one you do not know. He is the one who comes after me, the
straps of whose sandals I am not worthy to untie." This all
happened at Bethany on the other side of the Jordan, where
John was baptizing.
(JOHN 1:26–28)

John the Baptist brings clarity to their line of questioning by answering a more important question: "How?" So from "Why then?" in the previous verse he moves them to "How then?," and he answers with, "I baptize with water." He introduces the Jews to a new era. A public display of spiritual cleansing. An outward sign of an inward conversion. All who chose to believe would be cleansed of their sins as they responded to the Spirit's invitation of baptism. Water submersion to declare they had repentant hearts and believed their Messiah was here. A new era had indeed begun.

As soon as John the Baptist answers the question, he moves on and turns the crowd's attention to the Messiah who is already standing among them. No one yet knows who He is, but John wants everyone to prepare their hearts to recognize the One when they see Him, so he directs their attention to One who is mightier than he, to One whose shoes he is unworthy to untie.

John clarifies that while he baptizes with water, someOne far more important than he is coming. SomeOne he's not worthy to serve, someOne we are unworthy to have among us because He will come to baptize with the Holy Spirit. We read his words here:

> And this was his message: "After me comes the one more powerful than I, the straps of whose sandals I am not worthy to stoop down and untie. I baptize you with water, but he will baptize you with the Holy Spirit." (Mark 1:7–8)

John the Baptist was meek and humble. He pointed not to his own credentials or worthiness to baptize, but instead pointed out his unworthiness to serve Jesus. He was not even worthy to "stoop down and untie" Jesus' sandals. Stooping and untying sandals being an act of submissive and lowly admission, John was saying he was unworthy of even this because he was unworthy of being in the presence of God. John was trying to help us understand the very significance His presence has on us. It is as if he's saying: *to be standing in the same location, to be walking the same streets, and to be sharing the same oxygen as Jesus is of profound significance. We are on holy ground, let's not ignore this.*

In the movie *The Case for Christ*, Lee Strobel, an atheist searching for evidence to disprove Jesus' divinity, is confronted by Kenny London, a Christian co-worker who challenges him by reminding him of this one great quote from his hero, C. S. Lewis, "Christianity is a statement which, if false, is of no importance, and, if true, of infinite importance. The one thing it cannot be is moderately important."[1]

John the Baptist is calling the Jews to look to Jesus. Today we are being called to look to Jesus. It is of infinite importance that His attention is on us, so let's turn our attention to Him.

1. Lewis, *God in the Dock,* 101.

Pray the prayer you feel most in your heart today. Below are two suggestions.

Dear Father,
I find that so often I care so much about the attention that I get from others. It makes me feel seen and special when I am acknowledged. But Jesus, help me to only desire Your attention. And may my only concern be to serve You and honor You with my life. And as I look to You, may all of the attention around me become of less importance.
In Jesus' Name, Amen.

Dear God,
If You are real, please show me. Give me the eyes and ears to see You and to hear You. I am skeptical and I don't want to be anymore. I want to know for sure that You are who the Bible says You are. Please show me the truth of who Jesus is.
Amen.

Reflect ~

Sometimes we just need to be reminded of the importance of Jesus' life here on Earth. Think about what this means for you. Why is it so significant?

His Word ~

Jesus answered, "I am the way and the truth and the life. No one comes to the Father except through me. (John 14:6)

~ *Seventeen* ~

MAY HE TAKE YOU FROM THE KNOWN AND COMFORTABLE TO THE UNKNOWN

I WONDERED WHAT HER new life would look like now that she was moving back home. My little sister, now an adult, was moving back home after a decade-long stint in Hollywood. The last time we lived together was when she was in elementary school and had dreams with no limits. And she pursued those dreams and would return to live in our home as she searched for where God wanted her next. Would acting remain in her future? Maybe her future would look differently than what she had hoped.

A few years ago, my sister and I had the chance to have a heart-to-heart. Something we both realized we had never done before. There are seven years that separate us. I'm the third child and she's the fourth. So there are no other siblings between us. When she was in elementary school, I graduated from high school, so we missed out on some crucial years of bonding. As a high schooler, I was too busy creating a social life to give her any time or attention. When I went off to college, she started her middle school years, and when I got married, she was in her high school years, so I was quite absent for those very important years in her life. We were both old enough now to look back and reflect. Quite honestly, we mourned that we had lost those precious years. But now, God was leading her into my home for a time. Would we rekindle our sisterhood?

Though these questions filled my mind and most certainly in hers, I knew that one thing was for certain: God had pursued her. He had found her and she could say from a distance, "Jesus is coming toward me." He came and rescued her when life became painfully difficult. She had been surrounded with gracious friends who loved on her and cared for her throughout her time in L.A. God's loving hand and His fingerprints were interwoven in the friendships He had sent her, and in the church that had led her to drink the Living Water and to feast on the Bread of Life: Jesus. Now what would come next?

It would become a time of healing and pursuing. Pursuing God's will in this next chapter of her life, in this next chapter where He would continue writing His story in her life. Oftentimes God pulls us away from all we know. He pulls us away from what's comfortable and known to a place where we can truly be transformed.

Transformation can be a painful and unappealing process, but when we allow Jesus to make changes in our lives, He ends up changing our eyes. He changes our hearts and He remakes us into people who become delighted at the sight of our LORD. Then we can shout out to all those around us, "Come and see Jesus!"

May He take you from
the known and comfortable
to the unknown and uncomfortable
that you may be made new.

COME AND SEE

The next day John saw Jesus coming toward him and said,
"Look, the Lamb of God, who takes away the sin of the world!
This is the one I meant when I said, 'A man who comes after
me has surpassed me because he was before me.' I myself did
not know him, but the reason I came baptizing with water was
that he might be revealed to Israel."
(JOHN 1:29–31)

Come and see Jesus because He comes to see you! Jesus literally comes toward John the Baptist. As He always does, He comes toward us. He searches for us and then arrives with great power and love and transforms us. As Jesus approaches John and sees him, I imagine their hearts, once again, connect as they did when they were in the womb. John is delighted at the sight of his LORD. John has eyes to see Him and calls on everyone around him to *Come and see.*

It is as if John is saying: *The final Lamb who will be slaughtered and ultimately sacrificed, is here. He is the Lamb sent from God who will carry and take away all of our sin. We no longer need to sacrifice and shed the blood of another animal—His own blood will be shed and He will be sacrificed ONCE and for ALL!*

John explains that He is the One he spoke about before. And though Jesus is showing up after John's arrival, Jesus is actually greater than him and from before time. So He has always been here.

Though John the Baptist and Jesus were relatives and born within months of each other, John states that he did not know Jesus. Meaning, he had not seen him and had not met him. Jesus was raised in His hometown with Mary and Joseph in Nazareth (Luke 1:26–27) and John was raised in his hometown with Elizabeth and Zechariah in the hill country of Judea roughly ninety miles away (Luke 1:39–40). Both lived to fulfill prophecy and to further the kingdom of heaven: John to humbly serve His King, and Jesus to serve His Father. And John would reveal Jesus through baptism.

God's will was to reveal Jesus through water. Water is symbolic in baptism as it represents the cleansing of our sin, the reNEWing of our minds and bodies now as fully forgiven children of God. The Jews were used to cleansing in order to enter the temple of God. But now, one act, one sacrament, would cover the rest of our lives. One cleansing for a lifetime with God. Baptism was not essential for salvation but was a public declaration of one's faith in Jesus. Something extremely brave and convicting for the first century Messianic Jews. So many of them were brave by stepping up to be baptized. Might we be as brave as them?

Dear Father,
today I ask:
"Fill me with your Spirit
Give me the mind of Christ
Give me the eyes that will see
Give me the ears that will hear
Give me the hands that will serve
Give me the mouth that will bless."[1]

Reflect ~

Just as John saw Jesus coming toward him, do you see Him coming toward you? Are you ready for Him to remove you from a comfortable place to transform you? Ask Him to prepare your heart to serve Him and to reveal Him to all of those around you.

His Word ~

Do not conform to the pattern of this world, but be transformed by the renewing of your mind. Then you will be able to test and approve what God's will is—his good, pleasing and perfect will. (Romans 12:2)

1. Talbert, "Base Camp," 20:11.

~ Eighteen ~

MAY MY LIFE REFLECT JESUS

THERE ARE PEOPLE WHO come into your life and leave a lasting impression on your heart. They are earthly saints of the faith. In their imperfections they seek holiness, and through their life's testimony you are drawn closer to the heart of Jesus. There are three women who have had such an impact on my life.

My late friend Amalita (Amalia de Hernandez) became a spiritual mom for me when I lived in Guatemala in my late teens. Her endearing smile warmed my heart every time I saw her. She never hesitated to go out of her way to pick me up for church on Sunday and then lunch afterwards. While far away from my family, she became a mom, spiritual leader, amazing chef, seamstress, and confidant to me. Her hardworking hands sewed the veil that I wore on my wedding day. The symbol that we are now one, forever, in love. My spiritual mom would be there on my wedding day and would ascend to God's glory a few years later, but the impact of her life on mine and many others, including her sweet daughter and sons, will remain in us forever.

My Tia Martita (Aunt Martha) would become a second mom to me during my childhood years and into my adult life. Her hands that would embrace me and caress my hair as I sat in church with her as a toddler would caress my hair as I laid in that hospital bed in Guatemala twelve years later. Her love and care for me would continue as a I started kindergarten. She would drop me off and pick me up from school. Her love and nurturing words would discipline me and instruct me to return to Jesus in my early adult years. Through her life, I saw a love and fire for Jesus I would one day desire for my daughters. Her dedication to His people would have no limits. As a mother and wife, I continue to admire her and have the honor of seeing her mission work in Panama flourish and blossom into a ministry that is impacting children and adults with the love of Jesus. Her love remains in me forever.

My sweet mom, Rosa Urizar, has been a spiritual pillar of love and hope in my life. Some of my earliest memories are of her snuggling me and singing verses into my ear. She's loved me fiercely and with an undeniable passion for the Word of God. During the very challenging middle school and high school years, one ear laid on her shoulder as tears trickled down her blouse, while the other ear listened to her wise counsel. I couldn't have imagined that one day I would remember these things as I raised my girls. I'm one year shy of entering the middle school years with both my daughters, and I think about my mom and all the ways I can be here for my girls when they feel hurt and fragile. My mom's testimony continues to reflect His fingerprints in her life. Through the many storms she has endured from childhood into adulthood, she has undoubtedly chosen to trust in God. And now, as a grandmother, we see her continue to minister to women in Costa Rica, Panama, and her local church. Her life continues to impact the lives of so many.

So I'm challenged: What might our world look like if we invest in the lives of other women?

As I invest in the lives of other women,
may my life reflect Jesus.

COME AND SEE

Then John gave this testimony: "I saw the Spirit come down from heaven as a dove and remain on him. And I myself did not know him, but the one who sent me to baptize with water told me, 'The man on whom you see the Spirit come down and remain is the one who will baptize with the Holy Spirit.' I have seen and I testify that this is God's Chosen One."
(JOHN 1:32–34)

From his very own mouth, through his very own eyes, John describes the beautiful account of his encounter with the Spirit from heaven. With all eyes on Jesus walking toward them, John recounts the miracle he witnessed when baptizing Jesus: the Spirit of God descending from heaven as a dove and piercing this world. John had a front-row seat to this glorious event when the heavens ripped open and God spoke.

> Just as Jesus was coming up out of the water, he saw heaven being torn open and the Spirit descending on him like a dove. And a voice came from heaven: "You are my Son, whom I love; with you I am well pleased." (Mark 1:10–11)

It is here that John the Baptist receives confirmation that Jesus truly is the Son of God. Because remember, John had stepped out in faith and had begun proclaiming that the Messiah was coming. John spoke about Jesus during a time when all the Jews were waiting for Him. And John runs ahead of Him and says: *He's coming, He's coming.* And so it is with faith that John baptizes Jesus and then receives the most visually sound and beautiful revelation: the heavens opening and God's Spirit coming down on Jesus, confirming that He was the Son of God.

Any fireworks show pales in comparison to this glorious showcasing of God's glory. The heavens opened and remain permanently open for us all. His Spirit lives in us, making heaven open and attainable for all believers. It is His goodness, His love, His hand reaching down to us. Jesus is the path that takes us to our

Father, that takes us to heaven. He's the stairway to heaven. When the Spirit descended on Jesus, it remained on Him. And it wasn't a one-time only miraculous act reserved only for Jesus, it was God sending the Spirit down to us, demonstrating how the Spirit so literally descends on us and remains in us forever when we choose to believe and receive Him into our lives.

Did you notice that the Father sent the Spirit at the beginning of Jesus' ministry? It was as if His baptism was the inauguration of a new era, an era when Jesus Himself would speak the gospel truth to us and of who He was and where He was going, and best of all, who we could become and where we could go because of Him. Our salvation and baptism are like a birthday, salvation being the inauguration of a new era in our lives: a life in Jesus forever with Him.

And now John the Baptist is able to add to his message, "I have seen and I testify that this is God's Chosen One."

Dear Father,
Thank You for sending men and women into my life who redirect my eyes to You. Help my life to reflect You in every area and at all times. May I honor You with my words, my actions, and my whole life. Help me to invest in the lives of other women and lead them closer to You.
In Jesus' Name, Amen

Reflect ~

Women, how wonderful would it be if we all invested in the lives of three women? Men, if you invested in the lives of three men? Might we impact His kingdom in such a way that an entire generation is moved to live for Him? Write some names down and ask Him to lead you.

His Word ~

My command is this: Love each other as I have loved you. (John 15:12)

~ *Nineteen* ~

MAY THE BRAVEST PURSUIT OF YOUR LIFE BE THE PURSUING OF THE ONE

WITH EVERY STEP I could hear his shoe hit the pavement behind me. I tried to run faster. The coins in his pocket rattled louder and louder. I didn't want him to catch up to me. My three-foot-seven-inch self wanted to outrun my six-plus-foot principal. I was in first grade and entering mid-year at Garfield Elementary School. This would be my third and last school that year. I had made my poor mom register me and pull me out of two schools prior to this one. I was dealing with some serious separation anxiety, and with every new school I attended, my parents hoped I'd stay. But this school was no different. The very look and smell of school made me want to run like the wind and never come back. The full-day schedule seemed eternal to me and I didn't want to be separated from my mom for so long. But little did I know that this school would teach me more than I bargained for. In reality, this school would turn out to be very different from the others.

As my mom drove away after drop-off, I would run after her car. There I was, a six-year-old runaway. Seeing her car drive away was like knocking the wind out of me. I could not breathe. I could not fathom being away from her. But then I'd hear Mr. Loeffler running after me. He never gave up on me. He would very gently and lovingly sweep me off the ground and carry me back to the office where I would be welcomed by the sweetest staff. They offered me smiles, candy, and sweet reminders that I would see my mom again in just a few short hours. Not really short, I'd say. I still hear Mr. Loeffler's voice, his words and promises that my mom would come back and that everything would be okay. Day after day, he ran after me.

The daily agony of dropping me off at school wore on my mom. I'm certain I caused her severe emotional trauma when running and screaming for her to come back. My feet weren't the only parts of me racing, my heart raced faster than I could count, and I'm certain hers did too. How did she not give up on me? She had never-ending stamina, or at least it felt that way, like I could keep wearing on her and she would not break. But everyone has a breaking point and she finally reached hers. The last day I ran after her car was the day I held on to her body so that physically she could not let me go. I smothered and clawed my fingers into her back so that she could not detach me from her body. But I held on so tight it made her fall. I heard her knee crack and saw her thumb bleeding from the painful fall. I had squeezed her so hard it had caused her to break down. Her tears finally helped me realize that my uncontrollable tantrums were causing her emotional, and now physical, pain. What had I done?

So my mom knew to pursue Jesus during this time. I needed to go to school and her prayers were all that she had to get me to stay. So she began teaching me the verse that would take me through so many difficult days in life. I would recite it every morning and every night as I anticipated drop-off the next day. "Have I not commanded you? Be strong and courageous. Do not be afraid; do not be discouraged, for the Lord your God will be with you wherever you go" (Joshua 1:9). A sense of bravery fell over me. I wanted to pursue Jesus in the same way she pursued Him. It was my first experience with faith and trust. And I just knew God could be trusted. So Mr. Loeffler no longer had to pursue me because I was pursuing Jesus.

*May the bravest pursuit of your life be
the pursuing of the One who pursues you.*

COME AND SEE

*The next day John was there again with two of his disciples.
When he saw Jesus passing by, he said, "Look, the Lamb of
God!" When the two disciples heard him say this, they followed
Jesus.*
(JOHN 1:35–37)

After being with Jesus, John comes back for more. John had waited his whole life to see Jesus and now that he had seen Him he "was there again" waiting for His Savior. I imagine him returning to the same location filled with excitement to see God's Son again. All John the Baptist ever wanted was for his message to lead everyone to Jesus. Now he could so literally point to Him and say: *Follow Him,* "the Lamb of God!"

The two disciples knew exactly what to do. They had learned about their Messiah and they knew He was coming. They were immediately drawn to Him and they did not hesitate. They followed Him. John the Baptist had taught them everything they knew about Jesus so when the time came to see Him, they had eyes to see and ears to hear. They immediately followed their one true Messiah.

John the Baptist led with his life. Through word and deed, John had drawn his disciples closer and closer to Jesus. They saw him pursue Him.

Sometimes we pursue things that we think are right for us. Running after my mom was a good thing, right? But not in that moment in my life. So Jesus pursued me through the loving arms of Mr. Loeffler. And until I pursued Jesus in my own heart, I was without peace and out of control. So my mom showed me, through her pursuit of Jesus, how to find peace and rest in Him, and not in her.

"There's more abundance in daily giving your presence to
one than daily diligence for the furtherance of hundreds.
It's more like Christ to go after the one than to go after
the applause of the ninety-nine."[1]

Dear Father,
Thank You that You always meet me in the storm and bring
me back to shore. Help me to wholeheartedly pursue You the
rest of my life. Your love and truth remind me constantly that
You are with me. May I never forget it.
In Jesus' Name, Amen.

Reflect ~

Who can you pursue today that needs to know of the love of Jesus? Maybe it only requires a small gesture for now, a smile, a few
words, a listening ear, a simple act. Ask God to show you who He
wants you to pursue and let God lead you.

His Word ~

Have I not commanded you? Be strong and courageous. Do not be
afraid; do not be discouraged, for the Lord your God will be with
you wherever you go. (Joshua 1:9)

---

1. Voskamp, *Broken Way*, 233.

~ *Twenty* ~

"THE WILL OF GOD WILL NOT TAKE US WHERE THE GRACE OF GOD CANNOT SUSTAIN US"

THEY SAY, "BE CAREFUL what you wish for." I didn't quite understand this until one of my wishes actually came true in the summer of 2014. As I sat there on my living room sofa after saying goodbye to my family, the reality of what awaited us made me excited. My family had just left after gathering to pray at my house for our upcoming month-long mission trip to Guatemala. I had prayed that God would send my husband, my daughters, and me out into the mission field. I could envision my girls singing and praising Jesus alongside children in Guatemala. I could taste the beauty that would come of this trip and the opportunities we would have to love on children. My mind focused on what we would give to those in need.

The morning I first prayed this prayer, I sat in the second row of my church sanctuary. I had never sat so close to the front, but we had arrived late after getting the girls ready for church and well, these were the only available seats. Oh, but now I know God had these seats reserved for us. I was thrilled when I heard the instrumental version of "Hosanna" on the speakers. I had been listening to this song almost on repeat for the last year. The girls sang it at home and pretended to play it on their guitar. Often I would awake to the girls worshipping in their room with smiles that just pierced my heart. This Sunday morning, I sang at the top of my lungs and felt the words penetrate my heart. In that moment, I wholeheartedly prayed, "Jesus, give me your heart for the broken and the lost. Send us—Tachu, me, and the girls—to love on those You love. Send us to the mission field so that my girls would learn to love serving YOU."

So we worked hard to memorize Psalm 91 as we prepared to go on this trip. We learned this psalm so we could pray for His protection over our family as we traveled. Little did we know that the girls would recite it to a group of forty orphaned girls who needed to be reminded of His protection. God would use our sweet girls to encourage and inspire other girls their same age.

From the moment I prayed that God would send us, to the moment we stood in front of those girls at the orphanage, God prepared the way for us. He opened a door through my brother-in-law to reconnect us with the orphanage I had visited fifteen years prior in high school. Some of the children I had visited back in '95 would now be adults working at the orphanage. And now, I would visit with my daughters so many years later.

I prayed, "Here am I, send me," and He did. This trip was filled with as much love, laughter, and God's grace as resistance, sickness, and heartache, but in spite of the challenges we faced, it was an unforgettable visit. We saw God's protection over our lives in so many different circumstances. But best of all, the idea that we would give by serving and loving, in the end, was given to us. Sure, we gave clothes, toys and lots of love, but ultimately, these sweet kids gave us warm smiles, tender hearts, unbounding love, and their unspeakable joy. And I realize that the miracle is this: When you put yourself out there, you become vulnerable to receiving His love and His embrace and seeing His power and glory. There is no greater joy.

"The will of God will not take us
where the grace of God cannot sustain us." [1]

1. Graham, "Billy Graham Quotes."

COME AND SEE

Turning around, Jesus saw them following and asked, "What do you want?" They said, "Rabbi" (which means "Teacher"), "where are you staying?"
(JOHN 1:38)

Jesus turned around. Our Savior stopped and turned to look at John's disciples, who were now His disciples. They were following Him, because you see, when you come and see Jesus, you see that He is really coming to see you! He is the great pursuer of our hearts. In the same way He stopped for the bleeding woman (I encourage you to read the story in Luke 8:43–48), He stopped to see and speak to these disciples. And He asks them what they desire. What is it that they want from Jesus? And they don't ask to receive anything. Wasn't having Him in their presence enough of a present? So they want to stay with Him for as long as possible. They don't plan to follow Him for only a moment, they want to follow Him forever. It is as if they are saying *Here am I.* In the words of Isaiah the prophet:

And I said, "Here am I . . . " (Isaiah 6:8a)

The disciples wanted more of Jesus. They wanted to walk with Him, dine with Him, to learn from Him. They did not want to let Him go. They truly became followers of Christ. These were the same disciples that would one day be sent to "go and make disciples of all nations, baptizing them in the name of the Father and of the Son and of the Holy Spirit" (Matthew 28:19).

They would live out not just the first part of Isaiah's words, but the second part too:

" . . . Send me!" (Isaiah 6:8b)

The disciples wanted to so literally follow Jesus that day and every day. When Jesus sends us into the world, that is when we follow Him best. His love meets us at every location and in every home and crowd we speak of Him. And it's important to remember that Jesus did not come so that we might only be impressed with Him.

He is not and was not a great magician who came to town with a knack for showmanship. He is and was the Great Physician and Healer who came to town to fill our cup to overflowing. He did not come to Earth so we would only be awed by His performance, but rather so that we would be changed from within. The miracle is this, that in impressing upon us His love, He would cause a dramatic change in us, and therefore, in those with whom we share Jesus.

When He sends you to speak about Him, He is sending you to cause a change in others, so He does not send you away from Him, but He sends you into Him. Isaiah understood this when he said: "Here am I, send me." If we want to follow Jesus, we must be willing to be sent. Sent into our schools, our offices, our communities, our world, to cause a change in others and walk further into Him. And we can rest assured that He will prepare the way.

Dear Father,
Oh, how I want to serve You. But I am scared. May I be willing
to say these brave and courageous words: "Here am I, send
me!" May I trust that You will prepare the way for me and
that You will be with me. Lead me, that I may cause others to
follow You and draw further into You.
In Jesus' Name, Amen.

Reflect ~

How might the lives of those around you be changed when they hear about your faith? God doesn't need to send you far away to make an impact in this world. Sometimes the very people in your circle of friends are the very people that need to hear about God's love. Ask God to make you brave in sharing His love. Then pray, "Here am I, send me," and wait for Him to send you near and far.

His Word ~

Give praise to the Lord, proclaim his name; make known among the nations what he has done. (Psalm 105:1)

~ Twenty One ~

THERE IS NO BETTER TIME
THAN THE PRESENT

THE FIRST TIME WE dined at Nick's on Main, we did not expect to walk out with full bellies, yet still wanting more. It was an inconspicuous restaurant sandwiched between two other businesses. How we didn't walk right past it, I do not know, but there it was: very few tables, and crowded with families, couples, and maybe some businesspeople. But what struck us right away was how it appeared there were only three parties in the entire dining room of this restaurant. The space was so small that tables were pushed next to each other so that a group of fourteen people filled just one dining table down the center of the room. As we walked to our table, we had to say "excuse me" after bumping into chairs and tables along the way. Once we sat down, we practically rubbed elbows with strangers on both sides. You could hear languages from all over the world fill the room. It was beautiful. How did we stumble upon this little gem?

We walked into Nick's with no expectations. That night, our very hungry palettes turned into very satisfied ones. With every bite of "nana's meatloaf" I think I closed my eyes. What was happening? I enjoyed food, but this was a whole new experience.

It only got better as we looked around and saw that everyone's palettes were just as satisfied as ours. You could almost hear people mumbling "Mmm, mmm. Delicious." Well, just when we thought things couldn't get better, we saw some desserts being served.

Was it possible that the best was yet to come? And then, nearly in unison, everyone in the room looked up in complete amazement. All eyes in the room met, and immediately we began talking to the couple to our right, and then to our left. The dessert menus came only after Nick, busy at work in the crammed and overheated kitchen, came out to greet us at our table. Because that is what it was. We were all dining in Nick's dining room and he made sure everyone felt comfortable and at home. He wanted to know who we were and if we were enjoying ourselves.

In a lot of ways, dining at Nick's reminds me of what it means to dine with Jesus. Jesus invites us in to join His earthly saints. We come speaking Mandarin, Spanish, or French, just as much as we come speaking fear, pain, and joy. We come representing the many different places we all come from. We come from Nairobi, Chile, or England and we come from poverty, sin, and hope. And when we sit before Jesus, we are all His and He is all ours. We sit with our brothers and sisters as we feast on the words of Jesus. In unison we look up in amazement and we praise Him for who He is. His Word is our sustenance that keeps us coming back for more. Is it possible to be filled to the brim, yet come back wanting more each and every day?

Our experience at this restaurant—or any for that matter—in no way comes close to the satisfaction we find in Jesus, but it can certainly remind us that our Father's desire is to be with us and to satisfy our every longing. As J.I. Packer explains: "We have . . . made the point that God's end in all things is his own glory—that he should be manifested, known, admired, adored. This statement is true, but it is incomplete . . . It follows from the very nature of these relationships that God's happiness will not be complete till all his beloved ones are finally out of trouble: *Till all the ransomed church of God Be saved, to sin no more . . .* Thus God saves, not only for his glory, but also for his gladness."[1]

There is no better time than the present
to come and feast on His Word.

1. Packer, *Knowing God*, 125.

COME AND SEE

"Come," he replied, "and you will see."
So they went and saw where he was staying, and they spent
that day with him. It was about four in the afternoon.
(JOHN 1:39)

"Come and . . . see." The very words of Jesus. His invitation to us all
to *come* into Him and *see* who He is. And the disciples are invited
that day, and every day to come, immediately. He does not put
them off until tomorrow or the next day. He wants them to come
right away, because He does not wait to invite us in, and He does
not want us to wait to come on in. There is no better time than the
present. And this is when we are all invited to come and see. Now.

If there was any doubt in the disciples' minds as to whether or
not Jesus was in fact the Messiah, all doubt would soon be laid to
rest. The disciples would spend their time with Jesus in conversation. Allowed to ask and clarify, the men would know the mysteries of who He is and what He is all about. And this is precisely how
Jesus invites us in today. Through His words in the Bible, we learn
everything we need to know about Him. In this book of John, we
read the account of the apostle John. And through it we have a personal letter from our Savior to learn more and more of Him. Every
time we read His words, we are invited to pull more out from the
mine: the Scriptures. And so we see what the disciples saw that
day. We read it for ourselves and we dine and move into conversation with our Messiah. We feel, we hear, and we see His words. It is
as if He is saying, *Come and see for yourself, my child. Sit and dine*
with me. Sit and see where I come from and where I am going, that
you may know where you come from and where you are going.

And just like that, the disciples accepted His invitation to follow Him to where He was going. They saw where Jesus was staying
for the night. They saw where and how He lived. So He showed
them His temporary walls of rest to ultimately make our hearts His
permanent place of rest.

They spent the day with Him, John noting the exact time, because when you spend the day with Jesus, you don't want it to end. It is never enough. But then we realize, we have eternity with Him. This is only the beginning. So time will be on our side one day. He owns the time and He sets it as He wills, and on that day that we are face to face with Him, time will no longer work against us.

Eternity is right there. It is just moments away. Our time now is to be spent preparing for it. Dine with Jesus today. Open the pages of His Word. Find yourself in the pages of the book of John, and ultimately, find Him. There is no better time than the present. So I leave you this verse:

> "Taste and see that the LORD is good; blessed is the one who takes refuge in him." (Psalm 34:8)

Dear Father,
Thank You that You desire to be close to me so that I may draw closer to You. Help me to dine with You every day. I want to learn the mysteries of Your Word and the depths of your love. In Jesus' Name, Amen.

Reflect ~

Do you open the pages of His Word to be fed every day? Our list of tasks and our busy schedules may never change, but by going to Him every day, we can be changed. Ask Him to help you carve out a time and space to feast on His Word and to talk with Him.

His Word ~

Come near to God and he will come near to you. (James 4:8a)

~ Twenty Two ~

LISTEN AND FOLLOW . . .
FIND, TELL, BRING . . .

HAVE YOU EVER BEEN invited to dance with someone? Maybe not recently, but when you were younger? Maybe a high school dance or a wedding? In my culture, most of us dance at a *quinceañera* for the first time in public. It's a beautiful coming-of-age moment. Sometimes you make up your own dance moves and other times you follow your partner's steps.

In some cases, dancing can be very personal and memorable. I remember dancing with my husband at our wedding. As we slow danced he looked into my eyes, smiling as tears ran down both of our cheeks. We were so in love. So ready to start our lives together after a very long-distance relationship. I would follow him wherever he went and he would follow me wherever I went. It was a relentless, passionate love where we felt we could not live without one another.

We were so young when we met. We were both nineteen and right out of high school. It was a wonderful time of new beginnings. College, work, our friendship. I was taking a semester off to teach English in Guatemala to third grade students. I met my husband during a time of breaking out of my shell and exploring a culture I had grown up learning about but had only visited a handful of times in my childhood. And now, I was fully immersed in the language, culture, and people. I was just a young girl living in a new country and I had met a young boy, who would turn into the man I would fall in love with and one day marry.

The day of our wedding, it all felt so surreal. We had survived a four-year relationship where two of those years had been long distance. A 3,000-mile gap between us for months at a time. The idea of never separating from him again felt so dreamy. I wanted to be by his side for the rest of my days. Grow old together, live out our dreams together, raise children together, travel, have deep conversations, go on dates. Wow this was the beginning of something I could not imagine becoming even more beautiful. But that it has. And though I could have never imagined that the bumps and challenges along the way would make us stronger and more beautiful together, the pain we have encountered both within our marriage and from external sources have helped create this unique mosaic of our lives. From our wedding to laboring and delivering our baby girls, to some heartache we have caused one another and the heartache of raising godly, loving, compassionate, and hardworking girls, to the not-so-happy days, God has made something beautiful out of our imperfect marriage. And we keep going because we love and we commit and we let Him make us beautiful together.

Jesus never married when He was on Earth, well not in the traditional sense anyway, but He certainly entered into a marriage with us, His Church, through vows and promises and commitment and faith. And I realize that my imperfect relationship with my husband is a reminder of Jesus' perfect relationship with His bride, His Church. And though our walk with Him will never be perfect, He will always be perfect and He will never leave us.

So I think about how I danced with my husband on our wedding day, and how I dance with Jesus everyday. I just follow His lead.

Listen and Follow . . .
And next
Find, Tell, Bring . . .

COME AND SEE

Andrew, Simon Peter's brother, was one of the two who heard what John had said and who had followed Jesus. The first thing Andrew did was to find his brother Simon and tell him, "We have found the Messiah" (that is, the Christ). And he brought him to Jesus.

(JOHN 1:40–42A)

We are told that Christ desires a personal relationship with us. We want to believe it, and while we want it for ourselves, it's hard to imagine that God in heaven would want or have time for us. Not to mention, how exactly do you go into a relationship with someone you can't physically see or touch? But maybe, just maybe, we really don't understand the depths to which He wants to be close to us and live in us. Until I saw myself in the pages of the Bible, I had not really grasped this notion in its entirety. It was head knowledge, but I needed to make it heart knowledge. In these verses, however, I find just how He pursues our hearts to get our attention.

And this is where we begin to see the Genesis story of the first-century church. Part of what Jesus' death on the cross established was that the new church would no longer worship in a temple. The Spirit would conquer the hearts of believers and the new temple would indeed be our bodies, therefore making us the church. So the apostles became the church as did all those who received the message of Jesus. But before this could be established, Jesus chose which men He would instruct to take His message all over the world in order to invite everyone to be part of the church. And even before these men would spread His message, Jesus would die on the cross, but the preparation begins here in these verses where we see how He calls His first disciples.

Andrew was one of the two disciples that responded to John the Baptist's invitation to follow Christ. With our eyes on Andrew here, we see that he heard and then he followed. Andrew wasn't wasting any time. He understood this great calling on his life. So he danced with Jesus. He did a two-step dance toward His Savior:

he *listened* and then he *followed*. And after dancing, the first thing he did was find his brother.

So he ran to Simon Peter and then he did a three-step dance toward his brother: he *found*, he *told*, and then he *brought* Simon to Jesus. An ever-so-personal dance. He had to share something this good with his closest ally, his brother. And it was immediate. No stalling. No overthinking. Andrew wanted Simon to share in the gift he had just received. He did not keep it all to himself, but it was like the psalmist said, come, "Taste and see that the LORD is good" (Psalm 34:8). And Andrew told Simon, "We have found the Messiah." But in reality, the Messiah had found them.

Dear Father,
I hear You calling me closer and closer to Your heart. You are revealing to me the depths to which You will pursue me into a personal relationship, yet it is so hard to stop to listen and follow. Help me to give You all of me: my attention, my love, my heart, and soul. Like Andrew, may I respond. And may I not be afraid to dance the three-step dance with those You place in my life: find, tell, bring.
In Jesus' Name, Amen.

Reflect ~

Do you believe you have been found and handpicked? Jesus has handpicked you for His kingdom to do His great work. Ask Him to reveal this to you as you follow His heart.

His Word ~

Make me to know your ways, O Lord; teach me your paths. (Psalm 25:4)

~ Twenty Three ~

HE SEES ME, EVEN WHEN I FEEL NO ONE ELSE DOES

I REALIZED I LIVED on the wrong side of the tracks during middle school, that crucial period of time when the size of your house and the city you live in is nearly as important as the clothes you wear. As a young child it didn't matter because I knew I lived in a warm, cozy, and loving home. I didn't care about the name of the city, much less our zip code. But when you take notice that no pizza place will deliver to your neighborhood and you're thirteen years old, you know it's not something to brag about.

From a very young age my mom and dad had expressed to me that I was extremely special. My mom would share the story of her pregnancy and delivery with me every opportunity she had. She had almost bled out with me early on in her pregnancy. In the final months, her pregnancy became so fragile that she had to skip out on a trip to Disneyland with my two older sisters to lay in bed all day with her feet up. She had a weak cervix, she told me, and I could have dropped at any time if she didn't lay and elevate her feet. Once I did come, she became extremely ill. Running a high fever, she was forced to stay in the hospital an extra week. I had gone home with my father to be cared for by my grandmother so my mom could heal. I can only imagine the agony of not being with your newborn baby in those first few days. It had traumatized her, so she made sure I knew how much she loved me.

So I grew up with this sense that I was so loved and so cherished by my parents and God who had saved my life at birth, but then I grew up some more and began to see the things that other friends had and that began to shape my perception of myself. I always went to my friends' homes after school—I wouldn't dare invite them into my neighborhood—so there was always this sense that what I had to offer wasn't good enough. How quickly the feeling of being special dwindles when you measure yourself by what you don't have.

As I entered high school and my social life became busier, I could no longer keep my friends from visiting my home. And the surprise was that my friends loved coming to visit me. Our home always had a delicious aroma coming from the kitchen, hospitality to spare, and loud, fun voices. Our 970-square-foot home felt more like a 9,700-square-foot home with the amount of friends and family that were constantly being invited in. All of a sudden, our humble abode became the central station for sleepovers, dinners, and nightly TV watching. I learned that hospitality was a matter of the heart, and not the size of your home or the condition of your neighborhood.

It would be this home where I would say goodbye to my parents as I traveled to Guatemala, as I left for college, as I left to get married, and finally after returning to live with them as a married woman, before I left to live in our first purchased home.

As a young girl I could only dream of living on the other side of MacArthur Boulevard one day. But many, many years later, God would show me that little ole me, from the wrong side of town, would one day become the mother of two darling princesses and would write about His great miracles and blessings in my life. With God, there is no such thing as unworthy, uncalled, or unwanted. He wants all shapes, sizes, colors, social classes, cities, and neighborhoods represented in His kingdom. He blessed me with friends who never rejected me, and taught me I had nothing to be embarrassed about.

He sees me,
even when I feel no one else does.

COME AND SEE

Jesus looked at him and said, "You are Simon son of John. You
will be called Cephas" (which, when translated, is Peter).
(JOHN 1:42B)

As Simon approaches the Messiah, the Messiah approaches him.
Jesus looks at him. Imagine: Jesus stops whatever He is doing, His
eyes turn to Simon, and He looks at him. It seems as if, in that very
moment, the world stops, and then He speaks. He tells Simon He
knows him. He speaks reassuring words that calm Simon's racing
heart. Jesus knows Simon by name, and He knows who he comes
from, his father, John. Then the unexpected happens to Simon, as
it always does when you meet Jesus. Simon gets a new name, "Cephas" in Aramaic, "Peter" in Greek, meaning "rock." I wonder, did
Peter think: *But I'm just a fisherman.*

A rock is a naturally occurring, solid mineral that lies at the
surface of the earth. We see a rock when it is exposed and not lying
under the soil or oceans. In their first meeting, Jesus is calling on
Peter to a life of outward and inward exposure to unveil the mysteries of God. It was not by his own merit that he would become
a rock. It was not by his own strength or by his own accolades. It
was a pre-decided-upon, chosen-by-God honor to be a witness to
the life of Jesus.

I have seen the most beautiful rocks when driving along the
coastal highways of California. Powerful waves crash straight into
the rocks, yet they are unmovable. Jesus was calling Peter to a life
of unwavering faith. He would become an exposed rock, unveiling
the truths of who Jesus is. His teachings would be grounded in the
solid gospel truth. No amount of rejection or resistance crashing
down on him would cause him to crumble or lose sight of His
Savior, because you are where you come from. And Peter came
from His Father in heaven and was called to a purposeful life of
strength, power, and authority.

And we might ask ourselves, *Doesn't Peter deny knowing Jesus*
three times the night He is arrested? But God does not allow Peter to
remain in that state of denial, crumbling to pieces and never again

standing up for his faith. Peter goes on to be a great leader of the church just as Jesus had told Him:

> "And I tell you, you are Peter, and on this rock I will build my church, and the gates of hell shall not prevail against it. (Matthew 16:18)

And we are reminded that Jesus sees us–the person He created us to be, not our shortcomings–and He invites us in. He speaks directly to us, the fisherman, the young kid living on the wrong side of the tracks.

So, listen: What name is He giving you? What great and mighty life is He calling you to live? And remember, it is not through our own strength or merit that we are called into His kingdom to do His great work, it is all because of Him, by Him, for Him!

Dear Father,
Thank You for seeing me, for seeing my heart, and for allowing me to be called Yours. Please help me to listen intently to Your voice and to the name You have given me. May I remember that my strength and life's purpose come from You.
In Jesus' Name, Amen.

Reflect ~

Have you felt inferior or unworthy because of your background? Share your heart with Jesus and let Him bring you to a place of feeling seen, loved, and worthy. And maybe encourage someone you know that has struggled with feeling less than.

His Word ~

Call to me and I will answer you, and will tell you great and hidden things that you have not known. (Jeremiah 33:3 ESV)

~ *Twenty Four* ~

WHEN WE MAKE INACCURATE ASSUMPTIONS ABOUT JESUS

HAVE YOU EVER JUDGED a book by its cover? Made assumptions about a person that turned out to be inaccurate? I have made this mistake more than once in my life and I wish I'd learn from those mistakes.

You know that awkward minute that feels more like an hour when you first walk into a room of strangers? When it feels like everyone is staring at you, so you start sweating profusely and you don't know where to fix your eyes in that moment? You observe everyone comfortably talking to one another and laughing and you're just the odd ball out. It was my older daughter's first day in preschool. We were the new family and were coming in for the pre-K class, so the kids and mamas mostly knew each other. I was nervous dropping Arianne off that morning. I wanted to savor every minute of that first drop-off at school with my first daughter, but my nerves overwhelmed me when I stepped into her classroom. It was there that I saw this one mom for the first time. She walked in dressed so perfectly with her hair in a bun and her gregarious smile. She was definitely the mom I wanted to become friends with. Her daughter was just as sweet and pretty as her mama. I was immediately intimidated.

As that first month went, I would see her at the school meetings and in the classroom. I had quickly sized her up and assumed that she was the popular, talented mom who had a successful career where she traveled the world and balanced work and life so effortlessly. Earlier that summer I had signed up to be the class photographer for the year. I was excited to use my skills since that was the best I could contribute to the school. Shortly after school started, I found out she was also a professional photographer, to add to her already long list of skills and talent. She was an unattainable level of super mom!

So being the very mature and adult mom that I was, I of course resorted to avoiding her as much as possible. I would never be good enough to be her friend. But I couldn't avoid her altogether since both our girls were in the same class, so I finally talked to her for the first time. I was surprised to learn we had so much in common. We both had two girls of the same age and we were the same age too! We grew up on the same side of the Bay and we both loved God! It was shortly after that our girls started having many playdates together and our younger girls ended up in the same preschool class as well. Soon enough we were having picnics at the park and a triple playdate (our four girls and their mamas).

That friendship blossomed over time and we made so many memories with her girls and her twin boys who came just a few years later. Since becoming friends, she and her family have moved to another state. Our girls miss and love each other and we relish the time we had together. Jen became my forever rockstar mama friend. I love her so much and can't imagine what preschool would have been like for our girls without her and her girls.

I realize that God places special people in our lives that forever leave their imprint in our hearts. I learned a great lesson from my friendship with Jen: to never make assumptions about a person without getting to know them first. I'd love to say I've never made this mistake since, but old habits die hard. I do, however, try and remember that I could be missing out on a whole lot of love and friendship when I make assumptions. I could forever be changed for the better when I let my guard down and let God lead me into a friendship like His.

When we make inaccurate assumptions
about Jesus,
we miss out on a life-altering relationship with Him.

COME AND SEE

The next day, Jesus decided to leave for Galilee. Finding Philip,
he said to him, "Follow me." Philip, like Andrew and Peter, was
from the town of Bethsaida.
(JOHN 1:43–44)

What an invitation! Jesus is putting together His team of twelve and there is no city too far or minuscule that He will not call His disciples from. We know that He travels from Bethany to Galilee, about an eighty-mile distance. And it is believed that it is on this journey that He pursues Philip. And we see that sometimes He comes to us through other people, like Peter came to Jesus through Andrew. But here we see Philip's unique story, a personal visit from Jesus.

As Greg Laurie observes, "The interesting thing about Philip, one of the Twelve, is that he was personally reached by Jesus himself. While Philip brought Nathanael to Jesus, and Andrew brought Peter to Jesus, no one brought Philip to Jesus. Instead, Jesus came right to him . . . Normally God reaches people through people, but this was an exception to the rule."[1]

I try to envision for a moment Jesus looking for Philip. He will not rest until He finds him. And then Jesus sees him. In that moment, Philip realizes that Jesus is there for no one else but him. And He invites Philip with these two simple, yet profound words: "Follow Me."

To give you some background, Bethsaida, the town where Philip, Andrew and Peter were from, was in the Northern region of Galilee. Galilee was not known for its high-class citizenry. The people were classified as inferior. Given their far distance from

1. Laurie, "Practical Philip," para. 1.

the temple in the religious capital, Jerusalem, geographically, their theology and religious practices were considered less pure and less holy. But Jesus had chosen to recruit His men from there, and this was not a foreign place to Him either. He too was from that area, having been raised in Nazareth, which is also in Galilee. The Father did not choose to make His Son wealthy, opulent, or one of the religious or political elite, because He chose to send Him to everyday, ordinary, God-fearing, loved-by-God people like Philip, Andrew, and Peter.

And we see that in Philip's story, God defies all social norms. He chooses from the ordinary, not the religious. And He doesn't just come to Philip, but He reaches him and says "Follow Me," to become one of His twelve chosen disciples.

I love reading this story because it reminds me that God's love is so intimate and personal. How is it that our infinite God can also be so intimate? He came to Philip. He pursued him and invited him in. What an invitation! And Jesus did not allow Philip's hometown to get in the way of choosing him. He did not allow religious or political barriers to interfere. So I'm asking myself today, who has God placed in my life to reach with His hope and love? Is it someone across social, religious, or racial lines? Is it someone across my fence, my street, my office, my city, state or country? Jesus chose these three disciples to follow Him into the greatest kingdom work on Earth. And He has invited me too. Who am I going to pursue to invite them in as well?

Dear Father,
You are calling me out of my comfort zone and into Your
warm and comforting arms. You want to use me to reach
people. I want to make myself freely open and available for
Your kingdom. Please calm my fears, correct my mispercep-
tions, assumptions, and judgments of others, and help me to
love how You have loved me, so that I may reach my neigh-
bors, co-workers, peers, family members, friends, and strangers
with Your love.
In Jesus' Name, Amen.

Reflect ~

Is there a person or persons God is leading you to reach out to? Maybe you've had some fears of the unknown. Ask God to help you remain brave as He creates opportunities for you to engage these people with His love, wherever it may be.

His Word ~

This is eternal life, that they may know You, the only true God, and Jesus Christ whom You have sent. (John 17:3 NASB)

~ *Twenty Five* ~

IN HIM IS THE ONLY GOLD MINE

WHEN MY HUSBAND AND I purchased our first home in 2004, we felt like we had stumbled upon a gold mine, though we could never have imagined the turn our hopes and dreams would take stepping into that loft. When the realtor opened that industrial-heavy front door, it was like the music started on cue, complete with angelic voices singing to our every step as the sun beamed in our eyes and as we looked at one another and in slow motion said, "This can't be real." We had to call our family to share the news!

Earlier that year, we had arrived in the Bay Area as newlyweds, with only $10,000 to our names. We were young and inexperienced and had yet to begin our long-term careers. We had left our very first home as a married couple, our jobs and our business back in Guatemala. We left a life in Guatemala City that we had built in a short two years, but it was ours and we had loved it. My husband's family and close friends had played such a big role in our journey that it made it so painful to leave. That first night in California in my parents' home, we thought we had made a seriously *big* mistake.

Even though I had grown up in California, it all felt so unfamiliar and new coming back as a newlywed. My parents opened up their home to us and helped us so much with the transition. We knew however, that living with them had to be as fast as temporary could be. Not because that's what they wanted, but more because we were young and eager to have a place to call our own. Well days turned into weeks, which turned into months, and neither of us had landed a job yet. It was so disheartening for my husband to be told day after day that his tech experience in Guatemala was not transferable to the US. Employers wanted to see work completed in this country. But that's the tricky thing about experience, you can't gain it until someone is willing to hire you. And that person turned out be a dear friend of the family's who was working at a tech company in San Francisco. Finally, we had received some good news, and then my job followed a few weeks later. Soon enough we were visiting open houses on Saturdays and Sundays in search of our new home.

You don't realize the power of credit until you have a big-ticket item you're trying to purchase and you can't find a bank to give you a loan. We had bought our car in cash so we hadn't quite realized the enormous impact my husband's report would have on us when it showed only a few months of credit history. This is the only time I was grateful that I had signed up for a credit card that first year in college, albeit barely making my payments.

But then came another reality. Purchasing a home in the San Francisco Bay Area did NOT consist of you finding a home you and your husband loved and could see yourselves, your future family, future grandchildren, and your future gray selves in and live happily ever after. Oh no. Homes received multiple offers, sometimes upwards of thirty as homeowners hoped for a bidding war. It's safe to say that many discouraging and tear-filled nights followed for several weeks. In hindsight, it did not take very long at all from the moment we landed at the airport to the moment we were handed the keys to our new loft. But in those moments, it felt hopeless. So when we walked into the loft that would turn into our home, our hearts dropped as we were in disbelief that a place so new and gorgeous could be within reach. Needless to say, we had found our sweet home where our first daughter would be born, marking the beginning of our growing family.

In Him is the only gold mine,
a love that keeps on giving,
a rich source of life.

COME AND SEE

Philip found Nathanael and told him, "We have found the one
Moses wrote about in the Law, and about whom the prophets
also wrote—Jesus of Nazareth, the son of Joseph."
(JOHN 1:45)

From yesterday's verse there is no need to wonder if Philip chose to follow Jesus. Jesus searched for Philip and Philip followed. And now Philip searches for Nathanael and finds him. Building this team of twelve certainly entailed a lot of searching and finding!

Philip finds Nathanael and eagerly shares with him who they have found. He tells him that they have found Jesus. Can you feel and hear the excitement in his voice when you read this verse? Go ahead, read it again. Philip had stumbled upon a gold mine and he was not hoarding it all for himself. He was going to share this good news with others. And if we think about it, in reality, Jesus had found Philip.

And Philip knows that he can't just say he found Jesus, so he says it's the one Moses had written about in the Law. And it wasn't just Moses who wrote about Him, but so had the prophets. And consider this: maybe, just maybe, Philip and Nathanael had known Jesus as a boy, because then he says, "Jesus of Nazareth, the son of Joseph." It looks like Nathanael would have recognized Joseph's name. Had they purchased furniture or items hand-built by Jesus and His father Joseph? The news of good carpentry work would have spread among the people into neighboring cities. And now Philip awaited Nathanael's response. How would he answer?

As in those days, Jesus is still calling on His children to follow Him. And with great excitement He anticipates your answer. This is good news! You don't have to search any longer for what you've been waiting for your whole life. You think you have found the Messiah, but in reality He has found you. The Son's brilliance shines on you as you enter the promised land, His arms. You dance to an angelic choir of voices praising the Living Messiah, singing *"holy, holy, holy."* This is so much more than a gold mine. This is life!

Dear Father,

I am tired of searching high and low for something only You
can give me. Please help me to lay aside all of the distractions,
disappointments, and sins that entangle me and keep me from
living freely in You. Today, I accept this gift of love You are
giving me, and I pray that I will always cherish it and honor
You through my life.
In Jesus' Name, Amen.

Reflect ~

Is there something or someone stopping you from following Jesus?
Join the great saints like Philip and Nathanael, and make Jesus the
center of your life. Ask Him to help you work through whatever is
hindering you from beginning this new life.

His Word ~

Whoever has my commands and keeps them is the one who loves
me. The one who loves me will be loved by my Father, and I too
will love them and show myself to them. (John 14:21)

~ *Twenty Six* ~

MAY LOVE BE THE
LASTING IMPRESSION

IT WAS AN AWESOME day at the beach on this gorgeous summer day. The warm breeze blew against our faces as the hot sand penetrated our feet. The weather could not have been more pleasant and neither the company more enjoyable. Our friends had given us their summer home for the week in beautiful Lake Tahoe. We had invited my parents and relatives to come stay with us as our family alone only took up one-third of the house. We filled the bedrooms and stocked the kitchen and began our summer vacation for the week.

As it goes with a house filled with kids and adults on vacation, we played lots of games. The kids laughed and cheered, as did the adults. On one of the nights the kids had gone to bed, the adults stayed up playing and chatting. It just so happened that election season was well underway as we were about five months away from voting, so it was on everyone's mind. And in some unintentional way, our conversation diverted and before we knew it we were talking politics. And while it may have started amicably, after talking until 2 or 3 a.m., it did not end well. I think it's safe to say no one should ever discuss anything even remotely personal or emotional past 10 p.m.. A lesson learned a little too late.

I think about our conversation and I wish I could go back and erase and modify, edit, adjust, lower volume, modify tone, increase love, decrease arrogance, and the list goes on. My God, why didn't

I stop? Why didn't I go to bed? Why didn't I just listen? Why didn't I just talk to You about how I felt? A very low point in my memory of regrets.

I have had many thoughts following this regrettable conversation from a couple of years ago. I suppose life teaches you whether you're willing to listen or not, and well, I learned it wasn't worth it. I should have never taken on the role of being the convincer. The world has too many of them and that is not a role I was ever supposed to take on. And thank God that I don't have to because can you imagine the pressure?

The words of Jesus play in my head over and over. "My dear brothers, always be willing to listen and slow to speak. Do not become angry easily" (James 1:19 ICB). Is it not easier said than done? But it is possible! And I have learned that listening comes more naturally when it comes from a place of love. I started calling it love-ALL-ogy, the art of loving like Jesus. To love like Jesus is to reflect Him, to not as easily fall into the trap of arguing or convincing someone to think the way I do. Instead, I practice the art of love and friendship so I'm able to see the other person through a sisterhood or brotherhood, the way Jesus sees us. And I begin to understand more deeply that indeed: "Love is patient, love is kind. It does not envy, it does not boast, it is not proud. It does not dishonor others, it is not self-seeking, it is not easily angered, it keeps no record of wrongs. Love does not delight in evil but rejoices with the truth. It always protects, always trusts, always hopes, always perseveres. Love never fails" (I Corinthians 13:4–8a).

May love be the lasting impression,
not pride and self-seeking arguments.

COME AND SEE

"Nazareth! Can anything good come from there?" Nathanael
asked. "Come and see," said Philip.
(JOHN 1:46)

Ouch! Not the response I imagine Philip had hoped to get from Nathanael. Philip had arrived so enthusiastically only to be met with Nathanael's snarky response. To give you some context, Jesus had been in Bethany, the Southern region that prided itself in its close proximity to the temple in Jerusalem. This region, called Judea, was the center of Jewish religion. It was a superior culture marked with Jewish sophistication. Racially, they were less mixed and therefore saw themselves as being purer. Linguistically, they were superior in language than their Northern counterpart who spoke an unaccepted form of Aramaic, with an accent the Judeans rejected. Judea, Bethany to be exact, is where Jesus had called His first three disciples. But now He had traveled up North to Galilee, His place of origin.

Now, Galileans didn't have it all that bad. They were not under the same Roman rule as the people of Judea. They at least had a native Herodian prince, and due to their topography and land, their natural resources made some Galileans quite wealthy.[1] Nevertheless, they were seen as inferior by the Judeans.

But then we read Nathanael's response. One would think that Nathanael came from Judea, the more prominent Southern region, but actually, Nathanael was from Cana, just slightly North of Nazareth. Both cities were in Galilee, so why did Nathanael respond this way if they were relatively from the same area? I can only conclude that within the Galilean region, the Nazarenes were considered the more inferior group. And before accepting an invitation from Philip, Nathanael found himself with a dilemma because he would not want to be associated with anyone from the "inferior" Nazareth.

And yet without any hesitation or explanation, Philip simply says, "Come and see." Confident that Nathanael will understand once he sees Jesus himself, Philip does not argue or rebuke him. He simply directs him toward the Messiah, who will take care of the rest.

I have to be honest, my heart is quite shaken up by this story. I have more often than not looked down on people for what I

1. Taylor, "7 Differences," 5.

perceived to be arrogant comments. And I see now, am I not being just as arrogant, if not, more? Philip knew it wasn't his job to convince or rebuke Nathanael. It was only his job to invite him to see for himself. And this verse comes to my heart, "But go and learn what this means: 'I desire mercy, not sacrifice'" (Matthew 9:13a). He doesn't say anything about being self-righteous because He wants us to be merciful. In other words, our love for our brothers and sisters should be far greater than our disapproval of their views. My God, where is my love? I'm convicted that I have acted selfishly and arrogantly to win an argument.

Dear Father,
Confessing my sins is a very difficult thing to do when I want
to hold on to my hurt and pain. But You are showing me a
new way of living. And You are showing me the areas of my
heart that need forgiveness and repair. Please forgive me for
my arrogance, pride, anger, and self-seeking ways. May I love
above all else wherever, whenever, however, and with whom-
ever I am.
In Jesus' Name, Amen.

Reflect ~

Is there a situation in your life, past or present, where you need Jesus to help you sort through your thoughts and feelings? Maybe there are feelings of anger and pride that you don't want to deal with. Ask Jesus to give you clarity and to help you get to a place of healing where you can love the way He calls you to love.

His Word ~

We love because he first loved us. (I John 4:19)

~ *Twenty Seven* ~

THERE IS NO BETTER WAY THAN THE JESUS WAY

I COULD SEE IT in her face, how devastated she was by my words. The last couple of hours she had put this funny video together for a friend. The smile on her face said it all. She was so proud of her work. She picked the music, edited the scenes, and added a sprinkle of love and joy. But in a few seconds and with just a few words, I had crushed her joy and excitement. And the worst part is that I justified it as constructive criticism. My words had cut right through her gentle heart. I wish I could have a do-over.

I get so caught up in not wanting to enable my daughters that I'm so quick to throw any form of grace out the window. It's a fear of enabling my children to become weak and to think that everything they do is deserving of applause or a trophy. I want my girls to learn hard work and that sometimes you win and sometimes you lose. Life lessons just the way I learned them. But it is such a narrow and one-sided way of thinking. Certainly, in order to avoid becoming an enabler, I don't have to become a critical and unpleasant monster, I just need to find the right balance.

So I think about this for some time and try to find the perfect recipe for the right amount of positive words balanced with the right amount of constructive feedback. And I realize it's actually more about bringing out the right amount of Jesus and the right amount of Mommy. And the perfect balance is bringing ALL of Jesus through all of me. It means reflecting Him. This is not easy and something that requires a lot of understanding. I think it looks something like this: coming into the room and approaching my daughter with love and care, being genuinely interested in what she has worked on the last two hours, acknowledging her heart in the process, and observing her face and looking for the excitement and joy she feels because she not only thought of doing something special for one of her friends, but she took the time to learn how to use a new program to make it amazing. She learned to install, edit, add, and remove clips and music tracks to render a digital film.

I can become so narrow-minded that I fail to see the big picture. My daughter was trying to include me in a project that was important to her. She was sharing and I walked right in and with a couple of words and probably some not-so-attractive facial expressions, trampled all over her joy, enthusiasm, and hard work. Did it really matter that the video didn't look HD or if it did not look like it was directed by Steven Spielberg? It was better: a home video directed by my daughter, written and performed by her friend. I had clearly missed the point.

The truth that hits me hard is that this isn't the first time I've done this to my daughters, and I know I've done it to others too, where I'm so quick to criticize and even go as far as making assumptions based on superficial observations. From one Facebook post or a couple of Instagram pictures, I think I have them all figured out. I've identified everything I need to know about them, or so I think I have. I've placed them in a box that checks off their political party, religion, frequented stores, diet preferences, personality, vacation favorites, social class, weight, and shoe size. I'm baffled, embarrassed, and quite frankly appalled. This introspective writing is really cramping my style. I think it's called conviction. I'm convicted that the manner in which I have handled myself has directly affected the way I respond to my daughters. Oh my God, help me!

There is no better way than the Jesus way,
conditioning our heart to look upward,
not outward.

COME AND SEE

When Jesus saw Nathanael approaching, he said of him, "Here
truly is an Israelite in whom there is no deceit."
(JOHN 1:47)

One would think that Jesus would have a thing or two to say to Nathanael after his comment in yesterday's verse. Maybe a lesson on love and acceptance. Oh, but Jesus hones in on his heart. How telling of the way Jesus sees us. "But the things that come out of a person's mouth come from the heart" (Matthew 15:18a). Nathanael's words pointed to the prejudice and pride that had taken root in his heart. Jesus needed to address his heart and the sin that was blinding him from seeing that He was the Messiah.

As with all of us, Jesus needs to heal Nathanael's heart. And Jesus acknowledges that Nathanael is being truthful, that he is not hiding his true thoughts and opinions about Nazarenes and where he believed the Messiah would come from. In essence, Nathanael is saying: my Messiah will not come from Nazareth. He will be a powerhouse King from a superior and powerful region. You can't expect me to believe that my Messiah is from there?

Nathanael had attempted to follow Jewish law. But no one followed it perfectly except for the One who could fulfill the law perfectly because He was without sin. Nathanael's heart showed he was relying on his own unrighteousness. And though he thought he was a great Israelite, he was not representing the new kingdom of heaven. It wasn't enough to be a Jew. For the warning is this: "For not all who are descended from Israel are Israel" (Romans 9:6b). Being Jewish did not make him a believer. He needed to believe in Jesus.

Jesus' response is so unlike the response I would have given. I would have wanted to lecture Nathanael and then certainly would not have called him to be a disciple who represents the Messiah. But let's think about it. If Jesus responded in the way I would have responded, quite honestly, he would have never called on anyone to serve as one of His disciples. No one would have been worthy of this great calling. And truthfully, no one is. But being with Jesus causes a transformation in us that we could not accomplish on our own. And there it is, it has nothing to do with how good we are or how hard we try to follow the law. We all have sinful hearts and it is only by His grace and mercy that we are called to serve Him. So He chooses to call on Nathanael to be His disciple. Nathanael does not believe that Jesus, the Messiah, could come from Nazareth, but he follows Philip and comes to see Jesus anyway. And that is a good thing. As Joseph Exell puts it, "Being with Jesus ought to enlarge the most narrow mind: it enlarged Nathanael's, he was certainly narrow."[1]

Jesus did not call on the perfect to serve on their own, but rather on the imperfect to serve alongside Him. It is then that the narrow enlarges, the closed off opens up, the high up comes down, and the stubborn surrenders. Thank God He changes us from within and doesn't abandon us because of our sins and weaknesses. So I'm challenged to ask myself: Shouldn't I see people through the lens of Jesus and not through the lens of criticism and pride?

Dear Father,
For far too long I have been a judgmental and critical person.
Forgive me for allowing the seed of negativity and a rejecting
tone to be planted in me. Please heal me of this despicable sin
and help me to see others the way You see them—with grace
and mercy, always.
In Jesus' Name, Amen.

Reflect ~

Are you often quick to react with a negative tone instead of responding in genuine love? Are there people in your life that you have been viewing and responding through the lens of criticism? Carve out time every day to spend with Jesus so that He would enlarge your mind from narrow to wide through His Word.

1. Exell, "John 1:47, " Nathanael. I. 1.

His Word ~

How sweet your words taste to me;
they are sweeter than honey . . .
Your word is a lamp to guide my feet
and a light for my path. (Psalm 119:103, 104)

~ *Twenty Eight* ~

I Can Hope Big

As a first-time expectant mother, I dreamed about all the amazing things that I would experience with a new baby in my arms. The tender love, cuddles, and giggles. I would listen to songs like "Somewhere Over the Rainbow" and I'd envision holding my baby girl tightly in my arms and dancing with her. It was a song of hope and a bright future, an endearing melody that spoke to my heart and senses every time I heard it.

But you never expect the reality of the sleepless nights, the secluded hours that turn into days and then weeks, the constant feeding, and the endless laundry. A twenty-four-hour day that is more like a round-the-clock triathlon of feeding, changing, washing, and then doing it all over again. I think the lack of sleep is probably the toughest to endure, and yet, motherhood is supposed to be beautiful, lovely, and joyful.

I wanted sunny days in the park listening as my baby slept and the birds chirped in the background. I wanted a perfectly loving relationship with my husband where we held hands, had picnics, and bonded with our new baby. But this was not part of our story at this moment in our lives. This sleep-deprived, food-deprived, shower-deprived new mom was in survival mode. I felt imprisoned in my own home and I blamed my husband for the freedom I felt he had. I could no longer leave the house when I pleased, or leave for work without worrying about my babies, bottles, napping, and feeding. My mommy heart felt like it could explode with all that I tried to hold together.

And I see the gift that I was finally able to unwrap, the gift of love from my Jesus. His love through my family, my loving and precious husband and daughters. I think that too often we are unable to look beyond our circumstances because the prison we are in so successfully makes us feel like there is no hope. But it does not have to be this way. When we take what seems like a prison of hopelessness to Him and instead become "prisoners of hope" in Him (Zechariah 9:12), we realize we don't have to stay in this prison. He can tear it down and through it remind us that He sees us, He hears us, and He knows us. No matter how hopeless our circumstances may look to us today, remember that nothing is impossible for Jesus. He "is able to do immeasurably more than all we ask or imagine" (Ephesians 3:20). So hope BIG!

I can hope big because He is big.

COME AND SEE

"How do you know me?" Nathanael asked.
Jesus answered, "I saw you while you were still under the fig
tree before Philip called you."
(JOHN 1:48)

I think of a woman named Hagar as I read this verse (read the beautiful story in Genesis 16). Rejected by the father of her unborn child and his wife, tangled in a web of jealousy, she runs away to escape the pain. She finds herself all alone in a wilderness of her own. In the desert, concealed from the rest of the world and likely without food and water, it is here that God reaches in and speaks to her. He hears her aching heart and He sees her troubled eyes. "She gave this name [El Roi] to the Lord who spoke to her: 'You are the God who sees me,' for she said, 'I have now seen the One who sees me'" (Genesis 16:13).

Nathanael is all alone under a tree. In a concealed and quiet place far from the crowds, Jesus sees Nathanael in the same way He saw Hagar. Is it possible that Nathanael is also heart-struck? Does he feel abandoned, imprisoned or discouraged as he cries out prayers to God while under the fig tree? Nathanael is taken aback by Jesus and he asks the question we would all be thinking. Still not grasping that this man is Jesus, he struggles to really understand exactly what is happening at that very moment he approaches Jesus. So he asks, "How do you know me?"

Imagine a stranger walking up to you, confirming they know who you are though you've never seen them before. Nathanael was a skeptic and he wasn't going to believe Philip right away without some hard evidence.

Jesus knows that Nathanael needed to *see* in order to believe. In the same way he reached Hagar's heart, by hearing and seeing her, he reaches Nathanael's heart. Jesus helps him see that He saw him all along. And there is something pretty amazing about seeing Nathanael under a fig tree, since it was a fig tree that Jesus used in His parable to encourage His followers to repent of their sins and bear fruit (read more in Luke 13;1–9). "But the fruit of the Spirit is love, joy, peace, forbearance, kindness, goodness, faithfulness, gentleness and self-control. Against such things there is no law" (Galatians 5:22–23). Would this be the same fruit that Jesus would produce in Nathanael's heart? Well it was under this tree he received shade and a private place to search his heart.

Don't we desperately need a place of rest, a place where we can retreat from life to sit and talk to Jesus? It's usually the toughest time to speak to God when we are heart-struck. It feels as though the walls of despair are closing in on us, leaving no room to breathe, let alone speak, but just as we see with Hagar and Nathanael, we can trust that God knows our thoughts and is listening to our silent prayers.

Dear Father,
Thank You because I now know that You see me, hear me, and
carry me in Your gracious arms. Please rescue me from a life
of hopelessness and eternal death. Please tear down the prison
that tries to take hold of my thoughts and life. I surrender all
of my worries to You, Jesus. Thank You that You offer me Your
gift of life. May I take it and live by it. Only to You my King do
I long to give my heart and mind.
In Jesus' Name, Amen.

Reflect ~

Do you feel imprisoned by your current circumstances? Do you
have a dream that just seems hopeless? Ask Jesus to release you
from this lockdown, and to free you from this place. He holds the
key to freedom.

His Word ~

Now the Lord is the Spirit, and where the Spirit of the Lord is,
there is freedom. (2 Corinthians 3:17)

~ *Twenty Nine* ~

THE LIES AND SINS THAT ONCE BLINDED ME ARE FAR REMOVED

"THEN YOU WILL KNOW the truth, and the truth will set you free" (John 8:32). But will it? Won't it just cause heartache and an excruciatingly painful revelation? My God knows that truth has a healing power that every aching heart needs, but first sin tries to devour you and tear your family apart. And you never think it will happen to you.

Addiction and lies hit our home like a grenade right through our hearts, but my father had been a dedicated, loving, present dad all of my life. What had changed? In my late high school years, my dad took on a new job with a very long commute and was given the graveyard shift at a candy factory. This meant sleepless nights and a daytime sleep schedule that his body would never adjust to. He resorted to drinking as he coped with this new lifestyle. But then the visits to the casino just a few exits away from his new job became a constant temptation. One visit turned to two, which turned to three, and before he knew it, it was just as much a daily ritual and necessity as was his job. First he gambled away his night's pay. Then his week's, then his month's, and, well, you get the picture. As we learned more, he told us that there were nights he would come home with up to $100,000 in his pocket. All the while, my mom was working overtime to pay for my younger sister's private education and turning over all of her earnings to my father. Now he was gambling away her hard-earned wages as well.

It all came to a screeching halt when he lost our family's home. The one we had grown up in. A humble abode to say the least, but a precious and memorable one. My father's confession hit me rather hard. I had always felt like the apple of his eye, so I felt angry and betrayed. But I quickly realized that while he had done this terrible thing, his love in my life as a child was no less impactful and important in that moment. So I watched my mom forgive him. I watched her broken and afraid, yet whole and with God's amazing grace, come back to him. My mom had been rescued more than once by her heavenly Father, and this would be no different.

And we all learned that addiction is a powerful force that has the ability to take over your mind and body. It's a secret addiction that is most harmful to you and those around you. It finds its way into your life ever so subtly, yet viciously. It feeds you lies, empty promises, and false hope. My sweet dad had fallen victim to this addiction and it had imprisoned him.

The day my dad revealed the truth is the day my dad began his journey to freedom. No longer imprisoned by the lies, but exposed by the truth, he began sharing about the life he had kept from us all those years. God strengthened him in that moment to share his big secret.

This is probably the hardest story to share but it's also the most beautiful one because the change that I had always wanted to see in my dad, came after the truth had set him free.

The lies and sins that once blinded me
are far removed and replaced with
His truth and His love.

COME AND SEE

Then Nathanael declared, "Rabbi, you are the Son of God;
you are the king of Israel."
(John 1:49)

As Nathanael approaches Jesus, he is not prepared to meet the Son of God. He still does not believe it is Him. So almost immediately Jesus confirms to Nathanael that He knows him, and Nathanael finally sees that Jesus has seen him all along. As he sat under the fig tree, Jesus heard his heart, his thoughts, his prayers, and Nathanael is overwhelmed by the truth: Jesus IS the Son of God! He is the king of Israel.

I see how Philip so graciously invited Nathanael to come and see. He did it with a solid conviction, a soft, yet passionate invitation. He didn't take no for an answer, but he also wasn't forceful. It was a nudge, a hand that reached out as if to say "trust me." And the result was a beautiful and powerful moment where Nathanael's eyes were opened wide and he was able to say these precious words to his King, "You are . . ." because He is "I am."

When our eyes are opened to the truth about, our hearts follow. We cross over from untruth to truth and it's a gift that can never be stolen or taken away from us. It's guarded in our hearts and it's anchored to our souls. The truth is planted and takes root deep within us. His gracious hands plant a garden so exquisite, bountiful, and colorful within us. The holes in His hands make room for our hearts to feel His pulse as He gently plants the depths of His love and truth in us.

My father's life was transformed when the truth came out. God's truths began to fill his heart and mind; you are loved and not abandoned, you are seen and not hidden, you are cherished and not rejected. Similarly, Nathanael is transformed when he is face-to-face with Jesus. Nathanael had presumably been an honest keeper of the law, but nonetheless, he is proud, and this sin is quickly revealed to him. The beauty is Nathanael eventually realizes the truth of his sin and reverses his attitude and perceptions about Jesus.

When we study the Bible, we come across the many saints of the faith and patriarchs like Abraham and Moses. And then there are others like David and Jonah. All of them were men with extreme and great power whom God used to impact cities and great nations. Collectively they made many mistakes, yet they were chosen men. My father returned to His first love: Jesus. And it goes without saying that watching him immerse himself in God's Word and in His kingdom work has been an honor and a joy like no other. God allowed our hearts to sincerely forgive my father and to love him in spite of his errors. Because you see, we all have them. And we all need grace and mercy overflowing in our lives. Praise God that He forgives us. But first, He reminds us that He sees us with eyes of great love and tender mercy. And then He gently reminds us to look up, He is right there watching over us and working to bring us back into His arms. My God, You are a good, good Father. My sweet father has seen His Father, and his life is being renewed and transformed because of Him. Praise God!

Dear Father,
Your beauty overwhelms me. May I allow You to create an exquisite display of Your love and truth within me. May it be a pleasing aroma, a colorful garden that reflects You in every corner of my life. Thank You that Your truth sets me free, forever. In Jesus' Name, Amen.

Reflect ~

Have you allowed Jesus to plant His beautiful garden in your heart? Trespassers will only try to find a way in and will fill your heart with an unfulfilling void, so ask Jesus to fill your heart with His life-giving seeds of love, truth, joy, and peace instead.

His Word ~

Whom have I in heaven but you?

And earth has nothing I desire besides you.
My flesh and my heart may fail,
but God is the strength of my heart
and my portion forever. (Psalm 73:25–26)

~ *Thirty* ~

MAY MY WORDS AND ACTIONS NOT HINDER, BUT LEAD

MOTHERHOOD IS A PRECIOUS and most beautiful and delicate gift to women. Fatherhood is a sweet and fun and life-giving gift to men. Both are precious and infinitely fragile, a reality I've come to realize more recently. My eldest daughter is entering middle school in the fall, and I've become slightly more terrified by the minute as it draws closer. The changes happening as she becomes an independent woman are a reminder that life is about seasons. Life is in constant motion and constant change is inevitable. But I grieve the changes happening before my eyes. I look at her sweet face, through her soft and beautiful eyes and wish I could go back, for just a minute, to the days when she was an adorable baby girl who cooed and smiled at my every word, because now she has a mind of her own. It is a time of beautiful change, yet why doesn't it feel that way?

I have to be honest, I'm constantly offended when she doesn't need me or when she challenges my way of thinking. And the worst part is that for the first time in my life I have a chip on my shoulder ready to spew an answer like ammo on all cylinders. And it turns into anger and it unsettles me. So I realize I need help during this new season in life. I have actually ordered a book about responding when angry instead of reacting. I need it.

A few months ago, I had a very long appointment about some ongoing health issues and symptoms. What I thought would be a very thorough check-up resulting in a plan to heal naturally and holistically, turned into a three-hour therapy session where I was able to make connections between my physical and mental health. The connections I made pointed back to the very start of my health issues five years ago. It was mind-blowing. Our minds and bodies are so connected. God made us intricately and delicately and our emotions directly affect our physical health. I hate to admit it, but this led me to realize that I try to control outcomes in my life. From helicopter parenting to my personal relationships, I want to control the end result. And so, I embarked on a journey to release control to God. Truly let Him control all of my life so that I don't have to. Some of these behaviors were learned and some were innate. Regardless, this is something I had to spend a lot of time thinking about, praying about, and asking God to help me release my controlling habits to Him. Well, little did I know that admitting and learning to overcome anger would only be the beginning of a new season in life. Not allowing someone else's response to make me go from 0 to 100 in two seconds flat.

And motherhood, well it's the gift that keeps on giving because my daughters are teaching me so many things about myself. And I want to be a good mom to them. I want to be the mom God designed me to be, not the mom my emotions sometimes lead me to be, but as hard as I try to change and become a better mom, I realize that it doesn't actually work. I can walk into a situation and be as positive as possible, ready to remain that way, and yet very quickly revert back to my angry and controlling ways. But He teaches me. The Spirit speaks to me. A tree cannot produce a fruit unless it is deeply rooted. Likewise, the fruit of the Spirit cannot grow in us if we are not rooted in Him. Some of the fruit that the Spirit produces is love, kindness, gentleness and self-control. The Spirit produces a fruit we cannot produce. So in that moment of weakness we must cry out, "help me Jesus!" And in that moment of anger remember: I can't, He never said I could, He can, He always said He would. So the God Who spoke creation into existence speaks truth and love into my soul.

May my words and actions not hinder,
but lead my daughters to the arms of Jesus.

COME AND SEE

Jesus said, "You believe because I told you I saw you under the
fig tree. You will see greater things than that." He then added,
"Very truly I tell you, you will see heaven open, and the angels
of God ascending and descending on the Son of Man."
(JOHN 1:50)

Nathanael believed because he saw hard evidence. Jesus gave him what he needed in order to believe. Maybe Jesus wanted Nathanael to see Him and know who He was right away, but Nathanael walked into this encounter already predisposed to the belief that, "Can anything good come from [Nazareth]?" Nazareth was Jesus' childhood home, so we see that something great can come from there. Something groundbreaking and soul-penetrating did come from there, because out of the unexpected He births the unimaginable.

And Jesus promises Nathanael that knowing and seeing him is not the greatest miracle he will encounter. He promises that he will see far "greater things than that," things that will cause his jaw to drop and his senses to be altered. Jesus then promises him a very intimate and particular event in his life. And it's not anything that Nathanael could have imagined. Jesus promises him that he will see the heavens rip open and the angels of God surrounding Jesus, meaning Nathanael would later see Jesus being taken into heaven during His ascension. In other words, he would see Jesus perform His final miracle while in the presence of His people here on Earth.

Now here we are two millennia later. How many great things have we seen? Jesus' miracles did not end on that day, they only began. The Bible documents many of the miracles performed by the disciples. And I ask myself: How many more would believe, like Nathanael, if they saw hard evidence of miracles being performed today?

And I see that Jesus is telling us today, as He did Nathanael on that day, that being known and seen by Jesus is such a great-miracle, but seeing Him change us thoroughly, to reflect Him, is an ongoing miracle. Seeing angels "ascend and descend" on Jesus must have changed Nathanael profoundly and strengthened his faith. And today when we see Jesus answer our prayers, when we see Him do the impossible, when we see Him heal us, it changes us profoundly and it strengthens our faith—that is the ongoing miracle! Nathanael started out as a skeptic, but over the course of his conversation with Jesus, Jesus is gracious and gentle, softens his heart, and opens his eyes to see and understand what it all means. And still He promises Nathanael so much more.

Jesus is telling us these same things today. He is prepared to do far greater things in our lives than we have seen, things that will take us deeper into Him. The question is: Will we let Him?

Oh Great Father in Heaven,
Your majesty awakens us. Your miracles in our lives pro-
foundly touch our hearts and penetrate our souls. Thank You
that first You see us and then You move in us. May we have
eyes to see the miracles that You are causing in our lives. To
see the mountains that You are moving. To see the valleys that
You are removing. Help us to see that your grace falls upon us
every morning of every day of our lives. It does not run out,
but overflows infinitely in our lives. We want to see change in
our lives. We want to see You change us from within and from
without. Change us, Father, that we would see far "greater
things" in our lives and reflect You, to the glory of your Name.
In Jesus' Name, Amen.

Reflect ~

Do you want to see change in your life? It starts with seeing Jesus—His grace, His mercy, His love—and letting Him uproot your fears, control, anger, anxiety, and whatever else haunts you. Ask Him to help you relinquish all of these things and then allow Him to change you. He promises you will see "greater things" in your life.

His Word ~

Yet you, Lord, are our Father.
We are the clay, you are the potter;
we are all the work of your hand. (Isaiah 64:8)

Decision Prayer

I would love to invite you to give your life over to Jesus, and would love to walk you through the steps in inviting Him into your life, mainly your heart. There is no exact process or recipe except that you need to have a humble heart to invite Him in, and a spirit of repentance to understand that you are in need of a Savior.

Humility allows you to see His holiness and understand that the sin in your life doesn't allow you to have communion or peace with the Father.

Jesus came to give us the cure, a way in so that all might be made right with our Father. So Jesus willingly took your place on the cross. He willingly and lovingly wore the sin that separated you from Him. He reminds us here that: "God made him who had no sin to be sin for us, so that in him we might become the righteousness of God" (2 Corinthians 5:21). So not only does He forgive you for your present and past sins, but you become His righteousness, meaning, you become holy, pure, His child.

The invitation to receive His gift is completely yours. If you believe in Him and receive Him, you become His child forever.

And now, you can invite Him into your heart and soul. You may pray the following prayer wherever you are, or simply talk to Jesus. It's a heart decision, so let it come beautifully and naturally.

Dear Father,
Thank You for loving me so. Father, I realize that I am a sinner in need of a Savior. Jesus' death on the cross for me saved me from judgment, wrath, and separation from You. Thank You,

Jesus, for taking it upon Yourself to pay for my sin-debt. I believe in You and want to receive Your eternal gift of salvation. Please cleanse my heart of all my sin. Thank You that I am now forgiven and my sins forgotten. Lead me closer to You that I may grow in a deeper knowledge of your love for me and feast on Your Word.

In Jesus' Name, Amen.

> "They were filled with the graces of the Spirit, and more than ever under his sanctifying influences; more weaned from this world, and better acquainted with the other. They were more filled with the comforts of the Spirit, rejoiced more than ever in the love of Christ and the hope of heaven: in it all their griefs and fears were swallowed up."[1]

---

1. Henry, "Acts 2:1," para. 1.

BIBLIOGRAPHY

Exell, Joseph S. "Bible Commentaries: John 1:47." https://www.studylight.org/commentaries/tbi/john-1.html.

Graham, Billy. "Billy Graham Quotes." https://www.goodreads.com/quotes/199683-the-will-of-god-will-not-take-us-where-the

Henry, Matthew. "Matthew Henry's Commentary." https://biblehub.com/commentaries/mhc/acts/2.htm.

———. "Matthew Henry's Commentary: Isaiah 40:1." http://biblehub.com/commentaries/mhc/isaiah/40.htm.

———. "Matthew Henry's Commentary on the Whole Bible: John 1: An Exposition, with Practical Observations, of the Gospel According to St. John." http://biblehub.com/commentaries/mhcw/john/1.htm.

———. "Matthew Henry's Commentary on the Whole Bible: John 1:6: An Exposition, with Practical Observations, of the Gospel According to St. John." http://biblehub.com/commentaries/mhcw/john/1.htm.

———. "Matthew Henry's Commentary on the Whole Bible: John 1:19: An Exposition, with Practical Observations, of the Gospel According to St. John." http://biblehub.com/commentaries/mhcw/john/1.htm.

Laurie, Greg. "Practical Philip." https://www.crosswalk.com/devotionals/harvestdaily/greg-laurie-daily-devotion-jan-11-2011-11643928.html.

Lewis, C. S. *God in the Dock: Essays on Theology and Ethics,* edited by Walter Hooper. Grand Rapids, MI: Wm. B. Eerdmans, 1972.

MacLaren, Alexander. "The Fulness of Christ: Commentary on John 1:16." http://biblehub.com/commentaries/john/1-16.htm.

McManus, Erwin. "Really!?" *Mosaic.* March 11, 2018. https://itunes.apple.com/us/podcast/really/id74403741?i=1000406120836&mt=2

Packer, J. I. *Knowing God.* Downers Grove, IL: InterVarsity, 1973.

Patrick, Saint. "Saint Patrick Quotes." https://www.brainyquote.com/quotes/saint_patrick_190970.

Talbert, John. "Base Camp: Mission (Luke 10:1-3)." Filmed August 20, 2017. https://vimeo.com/230510825.

Taylor, Justin. "7 Differences between Galilee and Judea in the Time of Christ." https://www.thegospelcoalition.org/blogs/justin-taylor/7-differences-between-galilee-and-judea-in-the-time-of-jesus/.

Voskamp, Ann. *The Broken Way: A Daring Path into the Abundant Life.* Grand Rapids, MI: Zondervan, 2016.